Don Quijote
Dictionary

European Masterpieces

Cervantes & Co. Spanish Classics, Nº 1½

Don Quijote Dictionary

FOURTH EDITION

Compiled by
TOM LATHROP
Founder Member of the Cervantes Society of America
Asociación de Cervantistas
Sociedad Cervantina, Madrid

Cervantes & Co.

Introduction to Students

ONE OF THE THINGS THAT bothered me when I was a student was looking up words in *Don Quijote* was finding that they weren't in modern Spanish-English dictionaries because they were archaic; or they were there but only with modern definitions; or the list of meanings was exasperatingly long and it was hard to choose the right nuance. What I have done here is to prepare the dictionary that I would have liked myself when I was in *Don Quijote* class at UCLA in 1964. In this dictionary I hope to give you exactly what you need.

If you are using my edition of *Don Quijote*, you know that thousands of words are listed in the margins of the book. So why is this dictionary needed at all? In order to unclutter the margins, I listed the specific meaning of a word only *once*. If the word appears again with that meaning, it is not listed again. But if the same word has a new definition, this new meaning *is* listed. The meanings are listed only once, so, if your memory is like mine, you might need to look up some old words once in a while.

This *Dictionary* has 7800 entries and 12,000 definitions. I have tried to list all words that you ordinarily shouldn't be expected to know (**abadej**o *codfish;* **zaquizamí** *garret),* and some that maybe you should know (**padecer** *to suffer;* **raposa** fox), and sometimes I have given definitions for more common words, just in case (**manera** *way;* **nobleza** nobility). The first mention is listed with a part and chapter number (i.e., [II16] = Part II, Chapter 16). Words from preliminary parts of the book are so identified as well (i.e., [prII] = Cervantes' Prologue to Part II). Since

5

it is not likely that you'll be doing very much with these initial sections, words that are first introduced in the preliminary parts are also listed in the margins of the main body of the text the first time they appear there.

Adjectives are listed in masculine singular, even though they may not show that from in the text. Verbs are generally listed in their infinitive form, although some present and past participles are also listed, and some stranger, older forms are listed as they appear (**trujeron, veredes**) and variant infinitives are also listed (**escrebir, esgremir**).

Many times in this dictionary I list cognates, sometimes identical cognates, that are not given in the margins (**náusea** *nausea;* noble *noble),* just in case it you are curious if Cervantes used a certain word or not. Grammatical words (**el, las, mi, muy**) are mostly not listed, and neither are ordinary definitions of very common words (**libro** and **decir**, for example, are nowhere to be found). Sometimes when a common word has an uncommon meaning, only this definition is listed even though the word in its everyday meaning is seen many times (the only definition for **malo** for example, is *devil).*

In the headlines of the pages you will see references to where you are. The left-hand page refers to the first word in the first column and the right-hand page refers to the last word in the second column. Where it seems advisable, more than two letters were used in there references.

If you are dissatisfied with some of my definitions, look them up in a regular Spanish-English dictionary, which you should have in any case. The Cuyás is a really fine one, and the unabridged *Larousse* is also good and much cheaper.

This is NOT the first *Don Quijote* Dictionary. The first one, *Spanisch-Deutsches Wörterbuch zum Don Quixote,* will do you little good since not only was it intended for German readers, but its last edition was in 1821.

NOTE TO THE FOURTH EDITION:
As I corrected my new translation of the *Quijote,* I once again rethought a number of things and once again felt some definitions needed to be tweaked and also some errors needed to be fixed.

I hope I have given you enough in the edition and in this dictionary to make your reading of the *Quijote* manageable in its original from without needing to use a translation to help you along. If you find anything questionable, please don't hesitate to communicate it to me via e-mail (lathrop@udel.edu). I like it when readers find corrections. Of course I'd be even happier to hear any good comments you might have.

T.L.
Newark, Delaware
January, 2005

A

abad parish priest [I12], abbot [II25]

abadejo codfish [I2]

abadesa abbess [I52]

abajar to lower [I31], —se to bow down [I42], to lower oneself [II6]

abajo down [I6], after (in time) [II49]

abalanzarse to dash [I11]

abandonar to abandon [I40]

abarraganada in concubinage [II5]

abarraganado lover [II9]

abatanar to overcome [I21]

abatido disheartened [II26]

abatir to bring down [II43]; —se to submit [dedI], to swoop down [II22], — tienda to lower sails back [II63]

abc alphabet [prI]

abecedario alphabet [prI]

abeja bee [I11]

abernuncio I renounce [II35]

abertura split [II26]

abismo hell [I9], abyss [I14]

ablandar to soften [I20]; —se to relent [II35]

abobado spellbound [II25]

abolengo lineage [II47]

abollado dented [I25]

abominable abominable [II70]

abominar (de) to curse [I51]

abonar to vouch for [II1], to ensure [II22]

abono behalf [II32]

aborrecer to hate [I20]

aborrecible loathsome [II10]

aborrecido hated [prI]

aborrecimiento dislike [I21], loathing [II74]

abrasado burned [I5]

abrasar to set afire [I7], to burn [II65], —se to get burned [II41]

abrazado embracing [I32]

abrazamiento embracing [I23]

abrazar to embrace [I3], to grapple [I7], to clutch [I9]

abrazo hug [II13]

abreviar to cut short [I3]

abrigo shelter [dedI]

abrir: — camino to make way [II53], en un — y cerrar de ojos in the twinkling of an eye [II29]

abrojo metal thorn [II36]

absolver to absolve [I51]

absortar to absorb [prI], amazed [II25]

absorto absorbed in thought [I18]

abstenerse to abstain [I20]

absurdo absurdity [I48]

abundancia abundance [I2]

abundante abundant [II20]

abundantísimo very abundant [I31]

abundantísimo very abundant [II67]

abundar to abound [II11]

abundoso abundant [I48]

abuso abuse [I2], misuse [II43]

acá here [I18], **después —** since then [II1]

acabable transitory [II8]

acabado finished [I10], perfect [I21], dead [II12]

acabamiento end [I52]

acabar to finish [I1], to wind up [I28], **—se** to ten [II65]

académico academician [I52]

acaecer to happen [I15]

acaecimiento incident [I23]

acamuzado chamois skin [II46]

acanalado as if through a pipe [II22], grooved [II47]

acardenalado bruised [I16]

acardenalar to bruise [II69]

acariciar to treat tenderly [I37]

acarrear to carry [I34], to cause [II1]

acarriba above, up here [II23]

acaso by chance [I2], on occasions [I10], perhaps [II17]

acatamiento veneration [dedI], respect [I48]

accidente bond [II19], sudden fit [I23], fainting spell [II46]

acebo holly [I13]

acedo harsh [II10]

aceite olive oil [I12], oil [I50]

aceitera oil container [I17]

aceituna olive [II52]

acelerado hurried [I13]

acémila (de repuesto) pack mule [I19]

acendradísimo very unblemished [II38]

acento inflection [I27], sound [I46]

aceña water mill [II29]

acerado made of steel [II14]

acerca de about [I30]

acercarse to go/draw near [I14]

acero steel [I51]

acertadísimo very correct [II25]

acertado correct [I3]

acertar to happen [prI], to succeed [I3], to hit [I9], to guess [I24], to   find [I27], to be right [I50]. to succeed [II4], to achieve [II19], to guess correctly [II25], **— a** to manage to [I3], "could" [ded. II]

acetaban = aceptaban accepted [I26]

acetar to accept [II52]

achaque subject [I8], pretext [I40]

aciago sad [I28], ill-fated [II10]

acicalada shiny [II48]

acidente = accidente [I12]

ación = acción [prI]

aclamar to acclaim [II56]

aclarar to break day [I42/43], **—se** to clarify [I48]

acobardado low spirited [I8], unnerved [II17]

acobardar to intimidate [prI], to terrify [I27]

acocear to trample [II18]

acogemiento = acogimiento

acoger to receive [I11], to take in [I41], —**se** to resort to [I5], to take refuge [I16]

acogida welcome [I42]

acogimiento reception [dedI], welcome [I11], shelter [I17]

acólito assistant [II51]

acometedor attacker [I52], attacking [II1]

acometer to attack [I3], to undertake [I13]

acometimiento undertaking [II10]

acomodado reasonable [I1], appropriate [I22], settled [I24], accommodated [I42]

acomodar to accommodate [I2], to make fit [I1], to put in shelter [I2], to accompany [I2], to place [I22], to adjust [I27], to put away [I11], —**se** to supply oneself [I4], to make oneself comfortable, to accommodate oneself [I42]

acompañado follower [II13]

acompañamiento retinue [II44]

acompañar to follow [I4], to accompany [I8]

acondicionado trained [I18], **mal** — with a bad disposition [II65]

aconsejado ill advised [II29]

aconsejar to advise [I3]

acontecer to happen [prI]

acontecimiento event [I15], undertaking [I3]

acordado agreed [reI], reminded [I19]

acordar to remind [I27], to resolve [I5], —**se** to remember [prI]

acorrer to succor, help [I3]

acorrucarse to curl up in a ball [I16]

acortar to shorten [I30]

acosado pursued [I19]

acosar to harass [I31]

acostado lying down [I16]

acostar to put to bed [I35], to lie a person down [I46]

acostumbrado usual [prI], accustomed [I20], customary [I22]

acotación marginal note [prI], quotation [I33]

acotán falcon-like bird of prey [II10]

acotar to annotate [prI]

acrebillar = acribillar to pinch [II50]

acrecentar to increase [prI]

acreditado confirmed [II25]

acreditar to affirm [I28], to vouch for [I40], to confirm [I50], authenticate [II73], —**se** to affirm honor [I27]

acreedor creditor [II45]

acribar to sift [I31]

acrisolar to test [I33]

activo active [II8]

acto = **auto** sentence[I5], general public punishment [I26]

acuchillado holes (as if) cut by knives [I27], slashed [II1]

acuchillador slashing [II1]; quarrelsome man [II49]

acuciarse to hurry [I52]

acuciarse to hurry [I50]

acudir to go [prI], to run to [I3], to go [I18], to come [II4], to come to aid of [I34]

acuerdo concurrence [I6], awake [II12], memory [II67]; **estar en su —** to have one's wits [I41]

acuitarse to grieve [I2]

acullá over there [II12]

acurrucarse to curl up [II68]

acusar to denounce [reI], to advise [II4]

acuto acute [II38]

adahala fee [I31]

adalid leader [I42]

adamado feminine [II35]

adamar to adore [II1]

adarga shield [I1]

adarme a bit; literally, 1/16 of an ounce [II44]

adarvar to stun [II35]

adelantado *arch.* governor [I7], in advance [II25]

adelantarse to move forward [I8], to go in advance [I41]

adelante forward [I2], **pasar —** to go on [I6], **de allí —** from then on [I3]; *also* = **delante** [II2]

adelfa oleander [I13]

adelgazar to grow thin [II10]

adeliñado adorned [II32], dressed [II73]

adeliñarse to prepare oneself [II42]

adeliño manner of dress [II48]

ademán preparation [I30], manner [I3], gesture [II20], attitude [II25], **en — de** with the intention of [I11]

además besides [I2], excessively [I18], very [II71]

aderente = **adherente** accouterment [I2], connected to [I7], aide [I11]

aderezado adorned [I21], equipped [I47]

aderezar to repair [I1], to prepare [I11]

aderezo material [I35], trappings [II16]

adevinar = **adivinar** [I12]

adiós good-bye [II24]

aditamento inducement [II7], added obligation [II51]

adiva jackal [II68]

adivinanza prophesies [II25]

adivinar to foretell [I12], to guess [I40]

adivino fortune teller [II1]

adjunto addition [I22]

adminícula in small doses [II47]

administración management [I1]

administrar to administer [I50]

admirable astonishing [II35]

admirablemente admirably [I51]

admiración wonder [I13]

admirado amazed [I5]

admirar to amaze [prI], —**se** to be amazed [I3], —**se de** to wonder at [prI]

admitido accepted [I3]

admitir to receive [I14], to accept [I23], to allow [II23]

adobar to repair [I30], to clarify [I47]

adobo added flavor [II13], **en —** pickled [II47]

¿adónde bueno? to where [II24]

adondequiera wherever [II18], anywhere [II23]

adoquiera anywhere [II48]

adorar to adore [I11]

adornarse to adorn oneself [I41]

adorno attire [I41], adornment [II41], —**s** ornaments [I11], earned [I14]

adquirir to acquire [I28]

adulación flattery [I29]

adulador flatterer [aprob. II]

adular to flatter [II38]

adulterado adulterated [aprob. II]

adunio abundant [II50]

adversidad adversity [II3]

adverso unfavorable [I39]

advertencia judgment [I9], warning [I9]

advertido advised [I3], instructed [I7], noted [I33], quick-witted [I41]

advertimiento advice [I33], warning [I41], lesson [II12], lack of caution [II38]

advertir to be forewarned [I3]to advise [I8], to note [I10], to point out [pról. II]

afabilidad graciousness [I12]

afable courteous [I1]

afamado famous [I6]

afán distress [I19]

afanar to toil [I13]

afear to condemn [I28], to make ugly [II14]

afectación affectation [aprob. II]

afecto way [I34]

afeminado bland [I15]

aferrado grasping strongly [II45]

aferrarse to anchor to [I34]

afición eagerness [I1], affection [I3], fondness [I9], interest [I24]

aficionado devotee [I9]; liking [I48], fond of [II18]

aficionarse fall in love with [I45], to take a liking to [II19]

afinado having tuned [an instrument] [II44]

afinar to tune an instrument [II46]

afincamiento = ahincamiento ardor [I2]

afirmar to affirm [II24], **— el pie llano** to behave [II6], —**se** to make oneself fast [I4], to maintain [I11], to confirm [II72]

aflicción affliction [I42]

afligido afflicted [I17], distressed [I37]

afligirse to grieve [I8]

aforismo maxim [II47]

aforrado protected [I8], lined [II58]

aforro = forro lining [I47]

afortunado fortunate [I8]

afrenta affront [I3], disgrace [I16]

afrentado offended [I15]

afrentarse to be ashamed [I28]

africano African [II17]

afrontarse to confront [II1]

¡afuera! out! [I34]

agalla gill [II10]

agareno Mohammedan [II34]

agarrar to grab [II50]

agasajar to receive and entertain [I11]

agazapar to crouch [I28], to duck [II26]

agible feasible [I26]

agigantado gigantic [II36]

ágil agile [II7]

agilitarse to make active [II34]

agobiado bent over [I15]

agobiarse to bend over [II55]

agonía anxiety [I33]

agora = ahora [prI]

agorero ill-boding [I14]; superstitious [II22]; soothsayer [II58]

agostado withered [II12]

agraciado graceful [I18], genteel [I23]

agradable pleasant [I1]

agradablemente graciously [dedI]

agradar to please [I15]

agradecer to thank [prI]

agradecidísimo very grateful [II14]

agradecido pleasing [I7], acknowledged [I24], grateful [I27], favored [I39]

agradecimiento thankfulness [I24], gratitude [I12]

agrado affability [II18]

agraviado aggrieved [I13]

agraviar to harm [I8]

agravio injury [I1], wrong [I2], offense [I22]

agraz, en prematurely [II38]

agregar to add [II27]

agua rain [I42], **de — y lana** of little worth [II13]

aguachirle dish water [II20]

aguamanos water for washing hands [II31]

aguar to mar pleasure [I20], to water down [II51]

aguardador defender [I37]

aguardar(se) to wait [I2], to await [I4], to expect [II16]

agudeza subtlety [prI], repartee [I6], shrewdness [II33]

agudo sharp [I13]

agüela = abuela grandmother [I49]

agüela grandmother [II20]

agüelo = abuelo grandfather, *pl.* ancestors [II5]

agüero omen [I41]

aguijar to make haste [I34], to hurry [II14]

aguijón prick [I20], spike [I10]

águila eagle [II22]

aguileño aquiline [II14]

aguja needle [I28]

agujereado punctured [II55]

agujero needle maker [I17], hole [I33]

aguzar to sharpen [II58]

ahechar to sift [I31], to give [II25]

ahecho winnowing [II32]

ahí there [prI], **por —** over there [I1]

ahijado godson [I3], master [II14]

ahijar to adopt [prI]

ahincado zealous [I34]

ahincamiento see **afincamiento**

ahinco zeal [I15], insistence [I36]

ahíta overeating [II25]

ahitarse to gorge [I37]

ahogar to throttle [I1], **—se** to drown [I41]

ahondar to dig into [I33]

ahora... ahora [ora] whether... or [II21]

ahorcado hanged [II51]; hanged person [I25]

ahorcar(se) to hang (oneself) [I25]

ahorrar to spare [I6], to save [I10], to liberate [II24]

ahorrativo economizing [II40]

ahorro sparing [I48]

ahuyentar to drive away [II68]

aína soon [II49], **más —** rather [I18]

airado furious [I4]

airarse to anger [II1]

aire air [I3], wind [II14]

aislado isolated [II8]

ajedrez chess [I32]

ajeno of another person [dedI], irrelevant [I3], of another [I14]; **— de** void of [prI]

ajo garlic [II31]

ajorca bracelet [I40]

ajuar trousseau [II52]

ajustar to adapt [I28]

ál other, anything else [I2]

ala wing [I19], row [II34], **en —** in a half-circle [II60]

Alá Allah [I40]

alabado praised [prI]

alabanza praise [I3]

alabar to praise [prI]

alabarda halberd [II24]

alabastro alabaster [I13]

alambre wire [II74]

alameda poplar grove [II28]

álamo poplar tree [I51]

alancear to spear [I18]

alano great Dane [I6]

alárabe non-Arab Muslim[I39]

alarde, hacer to boast [II16]
alargar to reach [I13], to extend [I20]
alarido howl [II23]
alba dawn [I4], **al romper del —** at daybreak [I34]
albacea executor [II74]
albanega hairnet [I16]
albañil bricklayer [II6]
albañir = albañil bricklayer [I20]
albar white [II13]
albarda packsaddle [I42/43]
albarrazado reddish brown [II39]
albedrío will [prI]
albergar to reside [I23], **—se** to lodge [II22]
albo very white [II35]
albogue cymbal [II19]
albondiguillas small meat balls [II62]
alborotado turbulent [I5], agitated [I12], excited [I22]
alborotar to create disorder [I45], to excite [II11], **—se** to get excited [I20], to get worried [I40]
alboroto tumult [I21]
alborozado exhilarated [I4], disturbed [II45]
alborozar to delight [I47]
alborozo exhilaration [I2]
albricias reward [I31], good news [II65], **dar —** to congratulate [II25]

alcabala tax [prI]
alcabalero tax collector [II52]
alcahuete pimp [I22]
alcaide governor [I2], governess [II38]
alcaidía governor's office house [I5]
alcalde mayor [priv. II], judgeship [I2], friend at court [II43], magistrate [II27], judge [II66]
alcaller potter [II30]
alcance: dar — to affect [I14], **andar en los —s** to almost figure out, **ir a los —** to pursue [I52]
alcancía "piggy bank" [II20], incendiary bomb [II53], money box [II67]
alcanzar to reach, to attain [prI], to understand [I14], to obtain [I44], to overtake [II24]
alcatifa pew cushion made of silk of wool [II5]
alcázar palace [I2]
alcornoque cork tree [I11]
alcornoqueño cork *adj.* [II10]
alcurnia family [I13], ancestry [I22], lineage [I49]
alcuza cruet [I17]
aldabazo loud knock [II9]
aldea village [I2]
aldeana village girl [II10]
aldeano villager [I28]
aldegüela village *rustic* [I46]

alegar to allege [I38], to quote [II24]

alegoría allegory [II22]

alegrar to gladden [I14], —se to be happy [I18]

alegre merry [I13], happy [I40]

alegría joy [I6]

alejarse to go away [I18]

alemán foreign-made [II32], German [II54]

Alemania Germany [I49]

alemaña animal *rustic* [II29], Alemaña Germany

alentar to breathe [I45], to cheer up [aprob. II]

alerta, estar to be on the watch [II47], to be alert [II54]

alerto alert [II59]

alevosía treachery [I3]

alevoso treacherous [I3]

alfana strong horse [I18]

alfanje short, curved sword [I37]

alfaquí Arabic professor of jurisprudence [II67]

alfenique, -ñique almond paste [II1]

alferecía epilepsy [II14]

alférez lieutenant [I39]

alfiler straight pin [I26]

alfilerazo pin prick [II69]

alfombra carpet [II21]

alforja saddlebag [I3], —s knapsack [I20]

algalia civet [I4]

algarroba carob bean [II13]

algazara uproar [II20]

algodón cotton [I25], cotton ball [I4]

alguacil constable [II48], — de corte bailiff [II38]

alguna cosa something [I2]

alhaja belonging [I18]

alhelí clove pink flower [II41]

alheña, hecho una beaten up [pról. II]

alhombra = alfombra carpet [I50]

alhucema lavender [II67]

aliaga furze (thorny plant) [II61]

alias otherwise known as [II36]

aliento vigor [I10], breath [I5]

aligerar to hurry [II49]

alígero swift [II40]

alimaña animal [I50]

alimentar to nourish [I36]

alimpiar to clean [aprob. II]

alindar to border on [I30]

alisarse to make smooth [II41]

alistarse to prepare [I29]

aliviadísimo very relieved [I17]

aliviar to lighten [I19], to remedy [I24], to relieve [I49

alivio relief [prI]

aljaba quiver [II44]

aljófar seed pearl [I41]

allanar to subdue [I34], —se to level out [II52]

allegado follower [I37]

allende overseas [I1]

allí junto nearby [I10]

allombre = al hombre [I23]

alma soul [prI], heart [II35]
almacén warehouse [II67]
almagre red paint [II10]
almalafa Moorish cape [I37]
almario = **armario** cabinet [I46]
almeja mussel [I50]
almena battlement [I2]
almendra almond [II23], stone [I18]
almete helmet [I19]
almíbar syrup [II38]
almidón starch [II18]
almidonar to starch [II24]
almilla jacket [II1]
almirez mortar [II70]
almohada cushion [I8]
almohadilla sewing cushion [I28]
almohaza currying brush [II67]
almohazar to curry [II32]
almorzar to eat lunch [II7]
alojamiento lodging [II19]
alojar to lodge [I10]
alongado departed [I21], a good distance away [II27]
alongar to throw [II19], —se to go away [I17]
alquiler, de for rent [I8], rental [I29]
alquimia fool's gold [II6], alchemy [II16]
alrededor around [II27], — de surrounding [I13]
alrededores surroundings [I41]
altamente highly [II16]

altanería falconry [II30], highness [II30], —s heights [II41]
altanero high-flying [II22]
altar altar [II8]
alteración strong emotion [I28], quarrel [I50]
alterado rough [I41], angry [II1]
alterar to change [I33], —se to be upset [II70], —sele la cólera to become angry [II26]
altercar to debate [II41]
alteza high level [I24], loftiness [I41]
altibajo downward thrust [II19]l, —s ups and downs [II3]
altillo little hill [I18]
Altísimo God [II32]
altisonante high-sounding [I22]
altivez haughtiness [I12]
alto high-born [I25], high-sounding [I1], stop [I10], layer of fabric [II10], **de — abajo** all the way down [II63]
altura height [I14]
aludir to allude [II8]
alumbrar to illuminate [I4], to shine [I49]
alzado cleared [I50]
alzamiento revocation [I25]
alzar to raise [I3], to pick up [I21], to remove [I25], —se to raise [I2]
ama housekeeper [I1], mistress [I34], wet-nurse [II44]

amable loveable [I14]

amado beloved [I25]

amador lover [I14]

amainado lowered [II63]

amainar to take in the sails [I41],

amancebado cohabiting [I24]

amanecer daybreak [I7]; to dawn [I17], to arrive at dawn [I41], to wake up [I31]

amansar to tame [I42/43]

amantado draped [II36]

amante lover [I12]

amañarse to find a way [II13]

amaranto amaranth [II20]

amargamente bitterly [I34]

amargar to sting [II35]

amargo bitter [I13]

amargura bitterness [II18]

amarillez yellowness [II16]

amarillo yellow

amarra rope [II29]

amarrar to tie [II35]

amasar to knead [II33]

ámbar ambergris [I4]

ambición ambition [II32]

ambicioso greedy [I27], ambitious [II2]

ambos both [I20], — **para en uno** well-matched [I19]

amén de esides [I2]

amenaza threat [I14]

amenazador threatening [II1]

amenazar to threaten [I4], to menace [I8]

amenidad amenity [prI]

amenísimo very pleasant [II23]

ameno pleasant [II23]

amigo fond [II16]

amistad friendship [prI]

amo master [I4]

amohinarse to be irritated [I17]

amojamado dried up [II1], dry-cured [II23]

amor love [prI]

amoratado purple [II14]

amores amours [I1]

amorosamente affectionately [I33]

amoroso amorous [I11], affectionate [I42], gentle [II69]

amortiguado deadened [I24]

amparar to protect [I11]

amparo protection [I3]

ampo whiteness [II10]

anales annals [I2]

anascote lightweight wool [II38]

anca crupper [I3]

anchísimo stately [II23]

ancho broad [I2]

anchura breadth [I42/43], **a sus —s** freely [I49]

ancianidad age [II13]

anciano very old [I23]; old man [II23]

áncora anchor [I34]

andadura length [I35]

Andalucía Andalusia [I2]

andaluz Andalusian [I2]

andamio scaffold [II14], platform [II19]

andante errant [I1]

andantesca belonging to knights errant [I7]

andanza, mala bad fortune [I19]

andar to go [Ipról.], to act [I34], to float [II10], to walk around [II25]; a más — quickly [II8], — de nones to be vagrant [II49];

andar, cont'd. por — future [II73]

andariego swift [II1], gad-about [II1]

andas litter [I13]

andurriales by-roads [I29]

anegarse to drown [I14]

anejo a associated with [I15]

anexo a usual [I23]

ángel angel [I23], agua de -es perfumed water [II32]

angosto narrow [II6]

anguila eel [II18]

ángulo angle [II19]

angustia anguish [I20]

angustiado needy [II19], miserable [II48]

anillo ring [I10]

ánima soul [I4], fortitude [I3]

animal animal [I41]

animalejo small animal [I33]

animar(se) to encourage (oneself) [I19], to cheer up [II74]

ánimo courage [I3], mind [I13], courage [I23], heart [I45]; poco — faint-hearted [I20]; tener —

to have courage [I22]

animosísimo very courageous [I32]

animoso courageous [I32]

aniquilar to annihilate [I4], to humble [I22]

anjeo coarse linen [I16]

anochecer to fall asleep [I31], to grow dark [I2], to become night [II23]; nightfall [I2], to leave at nightfall [I41]

anotación annotation [prI]

anotar to annotate [prI]

ansí thus [I1]

ansia longing [I21], —s nausea [I17], torture [I22]

ansimesmo = ansimismo

ansimismo also [I22], likewise [I3]

ansioso in anguish [II28]

antaño yesteryear [II43]

ante before [I2], rather [prI]

antecedente preceding [I7]

antecoger to catch [II25]

antecogido followed [II17]

antecogiendo gathering [I19]

antes rather [I8]

antesala antechamber [II37]

antifaz veil [I26], mask [I37]

antiguo ancient [prI]

antípodas antipodes [II45]

antiquísimo very old [I21]

antojadizo unpredictable [prI]

antojarse to fancy [I3], to feel like [I8]

antojo fancy [I26], —s glasses [II19]

antojos de camino traveling masks [I8]

antojuno with eyeglasses [II48]

antonomasia call by nickname [I33]

antorcha torch [II53]

antropófago cannibal [II68]

anublar to cloud [pról. II]

anudar to join [II17]

anular to rescind [I10]

anzuelo hook [aprob. II]

añadidura addition [I1], **por —** in addition [I22]

añadir to add [I1]

añascar to confound [I20]

añejo wine [II3]

año, mal *see* **mal año**

añudado tied together [I35], withered [II47]

añudar to tie [I27]

apacentar to graze [I18]

apacibilidad gentleness [I47]

apacible pleasant [prI], peaceable [I2], affable [I30]

apaciguar to calm down [I24]

apagar to put a flame out [I16]

apaleado drubbed (person) [I4]

apalear to maul [I19], to snatch [II47]

aparadores, rodilla de dishrag [II32]

aparatos preparations [I39], festivities [I19]

aparejadísimos very prepared [II38]

aparejar to prepare [II4], —se to get ready [I8],

aparejos equipment [reI], trappings [I21]

aparente make-believe [II12]

apariencia appearance [I1], special effect in the theater [I48]

apartado distant [I14], out of the way [I27], separated [I40]

apartamiento isolated room [II9]

apartar to dissuade [I20], to put aside [II24], to lift up [II41], —se to separate oneself [I3], to withdraw [I4], to split [I42], to make way [I53]

aparte to one side [I6]

apasionado fond [I48]

apeado gotten off

apeamiento dismounting [II29]

apear(se) to dismount [I2]

apedernalado flinty [II35]

apelativo distinctive [I19]

apellidar to call together [I41]

apellido last name [I40]

apenas scarcely [I4], hardly [I2]

apercebido prepared [I41]

apero flock [I51]

apersonado good-looking [II48]

apesarado troubled [II64]

apetecer to crave [I27]

apetites reason [II14]

apetito appetite [I24], desire [I36]

apicarado mischievous [II32]

apiñado crowded together [II58]

aplacar to pacify [I35], —**se** to abate [I15]

aplacer to please [I39]

aplauso solemnity [I32], flattery [pról. II], applause [II26]

aplazado agreed upon [II56]

aplicación application [II73]

aplicado persevering [II22]

aplicar to apply [I11], to give [II51], —**se** to boast [I51]

apocado reduced [I16]

apocar to undervalue [I7], to diminish [I51]

apócrifo apocryphal [I48]

apoderarse to take possession of [II16]

aporreado cudgeled [I13]

aporreante combatant [I52]

aporrear to knock [I21], to pound [I45], to beat [II17]

aporrearse to punch oneself [II47]

aportar *arch.* to bring [I25]

aposento room [I6], space [II56]

aposta on purpose [II46]

apostar to bet [I10]

apostura neatness [I23], bearing [I37]

apoyar to support [I34]

apreciador assessor [II26]

aprehensión understanding [II1], apprehension [II14]

apremio constraint [I4]

apresurado hurried [II21]

apresurarse to hurry [II49]

apretado compressed [I28], dense [I40], cornered [II14], in a tight spot [II70]

apretar to distress [I2], to clutch [I4], to tighten [I20], to drive [II7], to squeeze [II17], to bite [I34]; — **el cerco** to lay siege [I34]

apriesa *arch.* in a hurry [I2]

aprieto difficulty [I20], awkward situation [II5]

aprisco fold [I50]

aprobación probation [I21], approval [I48]

aprobar to approve [prI]

apropiado suitable [II1]

aprovechamiento advantage [I49]

aprovechar to be(come) useful [I14], to be of help [I42/43], **no** — to do no good [I18]; —**se de** to make use of [prI], to take advantage of [I21]

apuesta bet [II62]

apuesto elegant [I17]

apuntado noted [reI], pointed out [I10]

apuntamiento agreement [II52]

apuntando aiming [I22]

apuntar to aim [I20], to prompt [I30], to write down [II3], —**se** to get angry [II19]; — **a dar** to hint at [I24]

apuñeado pummeled [I16]
apurado investigated minutely [I21], drained [I24]
apurarse to hurry [I42/43]
aqueso that [I32]
aqueste this [I33]
aquéste that one [I25]
aquí adelante, de from now on [I4]
aquistarse to be acquired [II42]
árabe Arab [I18]
arábigo Arabic [I9]
arado plow [I11]
arancel law [I35]
arañar to scratch [II7]
arar to plow [II53]
arbitrante adviser [II1]
arbitrio judgment [II1], will [II1]
árbitro arbitrator [I46]
árbol mast [I41], tree [I3]
arbolear to brandish [II68]
arboleda wooded area [II59]
arca chest [II20]
arcabucería musketry [I38]
arcabuz musket [I41]
arcabuzazo musket wounds [I51]
archiduque archduke [II29]
archivo archive [prl]
arco bow [I18], — del cielo rainbow [I13]
arder to burn [I7]
ardid ruse [II21], scheme [II56]
ardiente burning [I1]
ardimiento undaunted courage [I19]

ardite old coin of little value [I17]
ardor vigor [I2], heat [I12]
arduo difficult [I27]
arena sand [prl]
arenga harangue [I5]
arenoso sandy [I40]
arenque herring [I18]
argado bad move [II69]
argamasa cement [I11]
argentado silvered [II35]
argentería: hojas de — de oro golden sequins [II35]
argolla iron ring [I22]
argüir to argue [I49]
argumento argument [II40]
arista chaff [II39]
arma emergency [II53]; —s arms [II6], armor [I1], coat of arms [II18]; tocar (al) — to sound the alarm [I1]
armada fleet [I25]
armado dubbed [I2], armed [I2], with armor on [I29], ready [I48]
armadura armor [I18]
armar to dub [I2], to equip [I40], to put together [II20], to set up [II25], —se to arm oneself [I2], to be dubbed a knight [I2]
armas armor [I1], arms [I2]
armazón dubbing [I3]
armería armory [I49]
arminio = armiño ermine [I33]
armiño ermine [I2]
armonía harmony [I2]
armónico harmonic [II67]

arnaúte Albanian [I39]

arnés coat of mail [II22], suit of armor [II52], — **tranzado** articulated armor [II52]

aromático aromatic [I31]

arqueta small chest [I3]

arráez Arabic captain [II63]

arraigado of the landed gentry [II43]

arraigar to take hold [II74]

arrancar to draw out [I17], to pull out [I18], to pull off [I42/43]

arrasar to fill [II48]

arrastrado uncertain [II57]

arrastrar to drag [I25], —**se** to writhe [I41]

arrebatadamente hurriedly [II69]

arrebatar to carry off [I36], to snatch [I52]

arremangado rolled up sleeve [I18]

arremeter to attack [I4], to run to [I31], —**se** to dare to [II2]

arremetida attack [II55]

arrendador landlord [II52]

arrendamiento leasing [I50]

arrendar to tie a horse up [I35]; **no le arrendara la ganancia** I wouldn't like to be in their shoes [II1]

arreo continually [II12]

arreos trappings [I2]

arrepentido repentant [I27]

arrepentimiento repentance [I34]

arrepentirse to repent [I23]

arriba: medio cuerpo — from the waist up [I4], **de** — **abajo** from head to foot [I16], from top to bottom [I23]; **más** — **de** beyond [II24]

arribar to arrive [II6]

arrimado leaning against [I3], placed near [I4], to stick [II14]

arrimarse to lean [II32], to depend on [II44]

arrimo prop [I33]

arrinconado discarded [II62]

arroba 11.5 kilos [I9]

arrobamiento amazement [I27]

arrocado turned-up [I42]

arrodillado kneeling [I36]

arrodillamiento kneeling down [II10]

arrogancia arrogant thing [I4]

arrogante haughty [I4]

arrojadamente rashly [aprob. II]

arrojado bold [I14]

arrojar to fling [I3], to emit [I36], —**se** to throw oneself [II29]

arropar to cover [I17]

arrostrar to face [II16]

arrostrar to confront [I30], to look at [II16]

arroyo stream [I14]

arroyuelo little stream [I25]

arrugado wrinkled [II47]

arrullador flatterer [II41]

arrullar lulling [I14]

arrumbadas forecastle [II63]
arte condition [I18], art [I23], way [II16] —**s** cunning [I7], — **buenas** fine arts [dedI]
artesa basin [II32], trough [II53]
artesilla basin [II32]
artesoncillo basin [II32]
artífice creator [pról. II]
artificio craft [I6], ploy [I7], cunning [I34], **danza de** — artistic dance [II20], **figuras del** — puppets [II25]
artificioso ingenious [I11], play-acted [II8]
artillería artillery [I33]
aruño = araño scratch [II52]
arzobispal referring to the archbishop [I29]
arzobispo archbishop [I7]
arzón pommel [I20], — **postrero** rear part of saddle frame [II43]
asado roasted [II13]
asador spit [II20]
asadura entrails [I21]
asaetear to shoot with arrows [II24]
asalariado on salary [I21]
asaltar to strike [I2], to assault [I34], to seize [I41]
asalto attack [I23]
asar to roast [II20]
asaz abundantly *arch.* [I25], enough [I42/43]
asco nausea [I18], disgust [aprob. II]

asconder = esconder to hide [I28]
ascua ember [II10]
ascuras = a escuras in the dark [I16]
aseado clean [II16]
asegurar to guarantee [I4], to calm [I41], to reassure [I24], to make safe [I38], — **la conciencia** to clear one's conscience [II26], —**se** to protect oneself against [I1], to assure oneself [I36]
asendereado beaten [I25], overwrought [II9]
asentado established [II19]
asentar to note [I3], to fit [I7], to strike [I17], to settle [I1], to become [I7], to sit [I7], to seat [I45]; —**se** to sit down [II31]; — **una plaza** to begin military service [I39]
asesor legal adviser [II32]
asestar to aim [I38]
así thus [prI]; — **como** as soon as [I2], just as [I34]
asido attached [I23], grasped [I16], tied [II46]
asiento site [prI], seat [I24]
asimesmo = asimismo
asimismo therefore [I3], also [I7], likewise [I33]
asinino referring to **asno** [II33]
asir to grasp [I4], to hold [I22], to catch [II26], — **de** to hold [I3], to grasp [pról. II]

asistencia presence [I45]

asistente in attendance [II19]

asistir to be present [I34]

asnal asinine, that is "like a donkey" [II19]

asnalmente "on a donkey" [I7]

asno donkey [I5]

asolado devastated [II59]

asolar to destroy [I39]

asolver to resolve [II8]

asomar to appear [I8], —**se** to lean out [I41]

asombradizo shy [I19]

asombrado astonished [I35]

asombrar to terrify [II14], to darken [II39]

asombro dread [I32]

asomo trace [I52]

aspa windmill sails [I8]

aspado wound [I28]

aspar to wind [II47]

ásperamente harshly [II32]

aspereza hardship [I25], roughness [I42/43], —**s** rugged territory [I23]

áspero harsh [I14]

aspetator spectator *Ital.* [II19]

asqueroso revolting [I33], squeamish [II20]

astilla splinter [I5]

astillero lancerack [I1], shipyard [I41]

astrolabio old navigational instrument [II29]

astrología astrology [I12], —

judiciaria astrological forecasting [II8]

astrólogo astrologer [I47]

astroso ragged [I24]

astucias cunning [I47]

asturiano from Asturias [I16]

astuto crafty [I24]

asumpto = **asunto** enterprise [II2]

asunto subject [aprob. II]

asurarse to be burned [II41]

asustado frightened [II47]

atabal drum [II26]

atadillo little bundle [I40]

atado tied [I2], bound [I22]

atadura restriction [II18]

atajar to cut across [I23], to cut off [I33]

atajo shortcut [II61]

atalaya vantage point [II48], watch tower [II63], **en** — on guard [I33]

atalegar to hit with a sack [II14]

atambor = **tambor** drum [I18]

atañer to appertain [I2]

atar to tie [I4], to bind [I34], — **bien el dedo** to be careful [II7], **ser un loco de** — to me as mad as a hatter [II10]

atavío attire [II12]

atemorizar to frighten [II17]

atenazar to tear with red-hot pincers [II69]

atender *arch. for* to wait [I3], to attend [I7], — **a** to heed [I8]

atenerse to wait for [I21], to

abide by [I37]

atenido dependent [I38], sticking to [II44]

atentadamente discreetly [II1]

atentado careful [I16]

atentamente carefully [I44]

atentar = tentar to feel with the fingers [I18]

atentísimamente very attentively [I49]

atentísimo very attentive [I34]

atento attentive [prI]

atenuado lean [I9]

aterrar to destroy [I14]

atestado crammed [I3], filled [I22]

atildadura care [II47]

atildar to spruce up [II67]

atinar to figure out [I42/43]

átomo atom [II1]

atónito astonished [I9]

atontado stupefied [I24]

atormentar to torment [II8]

atosigar to poison [II10]

atraer to attract [I12]

atraillar to be on a leash [I22]

atrancar to bar a door [I17]

atrás behind [I37]

atravesado stretched across [I15], squinting [I52], pierced [II34], stuck [II35]

atravesar to go across [I23], to place across [II34]

atreverse a to dare to [I14]

atrevidamente daringly [aprob. II]

atrevidillo impudent [II24]

atrevido impudent [I3], fearless [I5], daring [I10]; impertinent person [pról.II]

atrevido bold [II51]

atrevimiento insolence [I3], daring [I38]; daring act [II11]

atribuir to attribute [I4]

atribular to distress [II60]

atronar to stun [I45], to deafen [II9]

atropellado hasty [II60]

atropellar to push through [prI], to trample [I28], to overcome [I33]

atrozmente cruelly [I18]

aturdido dazed [I3]

atusar to smooth [II32]

audacísimo very bold [I28]

audiencia court of justice [I3]

auditorio audience [I32]

aula palace [I52]

aullido howl [I14]

aumentar to increase [I27]

aumento increase [I1]

aun even [I35]

aún still [I6]

aunque although [prI], even though [I34], as though [I34]

aurora dawn [I2]

ausencia absence [I14]

ausentar to be absent [I14], —**se** to absent oneself [I20], to go away [I35]

ausente absent [I32]

auténticamente with authority [II72]

auténtico authentic [I52]

auto judgement [tasa II]

autor author [prI], authority [I1], perpetrator [I6], producer [I48], —**es** authorities [I2]

autoridad authority [prI], credit [I42]

autorizar to glorify [II17], to prove [I22], —**se** to find worth [II16]

avariento miser [II48]

avaro miserly [II6]

avasallado enslaved [I3]

avasallarse to submit to [II58]

ave bird [I8]

avecita little bird [II33]

avellana hazel nut [II10]

avellanado shriveled [prI], dry [I11], tanned [II50]

avemaría the Hail Mary prayer [I17]

avenir to happen [I2], to reconcile [I45], to adapt [I3], to act [II56]; —**se** to adapt [II11], to be together with [II53], to stay away [II62]

avenirse to be reconciled [I32]

aventajado superior [II14], **aventajado** excessive [II62]

aventajar to prefer [I37], —**se** to surpass [I4], to grow [II42]

aventura adventure [I1], risk [I33]

aventurar to venture [I8], —**se** to risk [I23]

aventurero knight errant [I2]; errant [I47]

avergonzado ashamed [II49]

avergonzarse to feel ashamed [I33]

averiguación verification [I15]

averiguado proven [I3], **no** — disputed [II19]

averiguar to find out [I2], to discover [prI]

avestruz ostrich [II23]

avieso adversely [I52], perverse [II62]

avisado clear-sighted [I27]

avisar to tell, warn [I5], to inform [I7], to send news [I42]

aviso counsel [I9], information [I14], announcement [I15], communication [I40]; advised [I15]; **sobre** — on guard [I24]

avispa wasp [II68]

avivado encouraged [I22]

avivar to inflame [I14], to encourage [I25]

ayo governor [I15]

ayudador helper [I35]

ayudar to help [I8]

ayunas, en fasting [II36]

ayunos without any idea [I48], fasting [II23]

ayunque = yunque anvil [I33]

ayuntado joined [I46]

ayuntamiento town hall [II52]

ayuso beneath *archaic* [II50]

azabache jet [II21]

azacán water carrier [I21]

azada hoe [II52]

azadón pick-axe [II33]

azar lucky throw in dice [I25]

azófar brass [I21]

azogado, temblar como un to shake like a leaf [II32]

azogue mercury [I31]

azor falcon [II30]

azorarse to become distressed [II33]

azotaina whipping [II35]

azote whiplash [I4], whip [I9], lash [I26]

azotesco pertaining to whipping [II48]

azufre, piedra sulphur [I4]

azul blue [I37]

azumbre half gallon [I10]

B

babador bib [II32]

babera beaver [I45]

bacallao = **bacalao** codfish [I2]

bachillear to jabber away [II7]

bachiller university graduate [prl]

bacía basin [I21]

bacín basin [I22]

báculo cane [I28]

badulaque jumble of things [II43]

bagaje pack-horse [II24]

bagarino Moorish rower [I41]

bailador twinkling (as eyes) [II1], dancing [II11]; dancer [II20]

bailar to dance [II19], **—le el agua delante a alguien** to see that one's wishes be seen to [II4]

bailarín dancer [II38]

bajar to lower [I4], to come down [I23]

bajel ship [I38], **— redondo** square rigged ship

bajeza vulgarity [I6], low condition [II5]

bajo low [I4], first floor [II61]

bala artillery shot [I33], bullet [II27]

baladro shout [I14]

balandrán short-sleeved cape [II62]

balazo gunshot wound [I38]

balcón balcony [I2]

balde: en — in vain [I28], **de —** for nothing [II5]

baldío idle [II48]

baldón affront [I17]

balido bleating [I18]

ballena whale [I31]

ballesta crossbow [I9]

bálsamo balm [I10]

bambolear to totter [II41]

banco bench [II63], bank of rowers [II63]

banda side [II63]
bandera standard [I18], flag [I40]
bandín guest bench [II63]
bando edict [II54], faction [I60]
bandolero highwayman [II60]
banquete banquet [I37]
bañar to bathe [I16]
baptizado baptized [I37]
baptizar to baptize [I37]
barajar to shuffle to cards [II7]
barata deal
baratija junk [II52], detail [II53]
barato deception [II45], tip [II49]
   hacer — to discount [II27]
báratro hell [II20]
barba beard [I7], chin [II41],
   hacerse la — to be shaved
   [I21], **a las —s del mundo** in
   front of the world [II72]
barbado bearded [I29]
barbar to put a beard on [II40]
bárbaro barbarian [I25]
barbecho plowed field [I25]
barbería barber's trade [I45]
barbero barber [I1]
barbilucio dandy [II1]
barbiponiente new bearded [II1]
barbitaheño red bearded [II1]
barbudo with a beard [II48]
barca boat [I20], ferry toll [I45]
barcada boat ride [II29]
barcino reddish colored [II74]
barco boat [II29]
barda fence [I17]
barniz lacquer [II17]

barnizado varnished [II62]
barra bar [I1], **—s derechas**
   without deception [II51]
barraganía concubinage [I11]
barranco ravine [I28], obstacle
   [II13]
barrenar to scuttle [II8]
barrer to sweep [II8]
barriga belly [I9]
barril keg [I41]
barro mud [II20]
barroso reddish [I27]
barrunto suspicion [I3], feeling
   [II26]
basa base [II6]
bascas nausea [I17]
basilisco basilisk [I14]
bastante sufficient [prI]
bastantemente sufficiently [II8]
bastantísimo quite [II19]
bastar to be sufficient [I1], to
   suffice [I33]
bastardo bastard [I7]
bastecido stocked [I19]
bastimento supplies [I12]
basto coarse [II5]
bastón staff [I13]
basura garbage [I15]
batalla battle [I1]
batallar to fight [II4]
batán fulling mill [I20]
batanado, anascote fine
   lightweight wool [II38]
batanear to thrash [I21]
batel dinghy [II1]

batir to strike [I18], to beat [heart] [I19]

bausán idiot [II11]

bautismo baptism [I42]

bautizar to baptize [prI]

bayeta flannel [II23]

beatificar to beatify, make a saint [II8]

bebida drink [I5]

becoquín cap with flaps [II48]

beldad beauty [I4]

bélico military [II34]

belitre vile person [I30]

bellaco roguish [I22]; rogue [I52]

bellacón rogue [II47]

bellaconazo villain [I24]

bellaquería roguery [I4]

belleza beautiful woman [I24], beauty [I29]

bello beautiful [I4]

bellota acorn [I11]

bendecir to praise [I12], to bless [I45]

bendición blessing [I12], thanksgiving [II8]

benditísimo very blessed [I21]

bendito blessed [I11], **agua —** holy water [I6]; saint [II47]

beneficiado priest [I11], **— simple** job with church [I26]

beneficio benefit [I8], kindness [I17], job [II49]

beneplácito blessing [II1], approval [II74]

benevolencia good will [II49]

benigno gentle [I11]

benito Benedictine [I8]

Berbería Barbary [II54]

berenjena eggplant [II2]

bergante scoundrel [II17]

bergantín brigantine [II63]

bermejo ruddy [II1], red colored [I10]

bermellón vermillion [I4]

besar to kiss [prI]

beso kiss [II13]

bestezuela little animal [I15]

bestia animal [I17]

bestión brute [II35]

besugo sea bream (fish) [II11]

Betis Guadalquivir River [I14]

bien good [prI], goodness [I11], good fortune [I40], **tener por —bien**, cont'd. to concur [reI], **o —… o —** either… or [I19], **— haya** good luck [I25], **— hayan** blessed [I38], **si —** even if [II26]

bienaventurado fortunate [II19]

bienes riches [I27]

bienestar well-being [II50]

bienhechor being kind [II58]

bienllegada welcome [I42]

bigote mustache [I20]

billete love letter [I24], letter [I40]

birlar to play [II19]

birretillo little cap [I27]

bisabuelos ancestors [I1]

bisunto stained [II18]

bizarramente elegantly [II34]

bizarría splendor [I27], elegance [II38]

bizarro elegant [I42]

bizco cross-eyed [I30]

bizcocho biscuit [I22]

bizma poultice [I15]

bizmado poulticed [I16]

bizmar° to poultice [I16], be poulticed [I17]

blanca copper coin, ½ **maravedí** [I3]

blanco bull's eye [I13], inexperienced [1,32], **de punta en —** from head to foot [I11], **labor blanca** hand work [II70]

blancura whiteness [I13]

blandamente subtly [II16], softly [II48]

blandear to wave [I40]

blandir to brandish [I4]

blando soft [I2], tender [I41], gentle [aprob. II]; **condición blanda** good temper [II24]

blandón holder [II69]

blandura gentleness [aprob. II]

blanquísimo very white [I33]

blasfemia blasphemy [I4]

blasón glory [II59]

boberías stupid things [II67]

bóbilis: de bóbilis, bóbilis free [II71]

bobo,-a fool [II3]; foolish [II20]

boca mouth [I2], **— arriba** on one's back [I16], **— abajo** face down [I41], **— abierta** agape

[I51], **en — de** talked about by [I41]

bocací fine buckram [II19]

bocado bite [I23], mouthful [I24]

bocina Little Dipper [I20], huntsman's horn [II34]

boda(s) wedding [I27]

bodegón wine shop [II71]

bodegonero tavern keeper [I8]

bodoque pellet [I16]

bofetada blows [I52]

bofetón punch [I25]

bogar to row [I22]

bojiganga jester [II11]

bola ball [I21]

boliche an old game [I18]

bollo bread roll [II50]

bolos ninepins [II19]

bolsa bag [I3]

bolsico small purse [II57]

bolsilla small purse [II58]

bolsón big purse [II20]

bondad goodness [I6], excellence [I33]

bonete cap [I37]

bonetero hatmaker [pról. II]

bonetillo night cap [I35], cap [I37]

bonico *diminutive of* **bueno** [I25]

bonísimo very good [I6]

bonitamente neatly [I18]

boquear to open one's mouth [II50]

borbollones, a [boiling] furiously [I50]

borceguí leggings [I37]
bordar to embroider [I31]
bordo, a alongside [I41]
bordón staff [I20]
Borgoña Burgundy [I49]
borla tassel [I38]
borra animal hair [II39], rubbish [II70]
borrachería absurdity [II13]
borracho drunk [I35]
borrador first draft [I23]
borrar to strike out [I1], to erase [I36]
borrasca tempest [I17], storm [I22]
borrica she-ass [I23]
borrico donkey [I5]
bosque forest [I4]
bosquejo rough sketch [I25]
bosqueril of the forest [II13]
bostezar to yawn [II17]
bota wineskin [I7], **—s de campo** or **camino** traveling boots [II44]
botana plug to repair wineskin [I35]
botecillo canister [I20]
botica apothecary's shop [I21]
boticario apothecary [II37]
boto dull [I25]
botón button on spur [II14]
boyero wagoner [I47]
bragas pants [II50]
bramar to bellow [I42/43]
bramido bellow [I14]

brasa hot coal [II17]
brasero coal fired table heater [I37]
bravamente fiercely [II58]
bravata bravado [II17]
bravo valiant [I17], fine [II12]
braza six feet [II22]
brazo arm [I1]
brebaje brew [I17]
breñas brambled ground [I26], thicket [I29]
breva fig [II35]
breve brief [I25], limited [II38], **—s** a few [I37], **en —** briefly [I17]
brevedad haste [I10], **con la mayor —** as soon as possible [I3]
brevemente quickly [II8]
brida long stirrups [I2]
brincador person who leaps [II32]
brincar to flit about [II33], to frisk [II38]
brinco leap [II25]
brindar to toast [II74]
brindis toast [II33]
brío force [I3], resolution [I19], energy [I37], dash [I1]
brioso spirited [I20]
briznas sparks [II41]
brocado brocaded fabric [I37]
broche brooch [II5]
bronca = ronca hoarse [I23]
bronce bronze [I2], bronze tablet

[I1]

broncíneo bronzed [I52]

bronco coarse [II49]

brotar to shed [II14], to sprout [II65]

brujo sorcerer [I25]

brumado = abrumado bruised [I4], perplexed [II48]

brumar = abrumar to crush [I24]

bruñido burnished [II17]

brutesco = grutesco grotesque [I50]

bruto irrational [I24], brute [I19]

bucólica pastoral poem [I24]

bucólica food [I24]

buen hora, a la happily [I3]

buena: de — en buenas all at once [II4], **— voluntad** good will [I33]

buenamente well [I16]

buenas artes fine arts [dedI]

buey ox [I27]

bufar snorting [II68]

bufete desk [prI]

buho owl [I14]

buido sharp [II23]

buitre vulture [I31]

bullir to boil [I50], **—se** to stir [I16]

bulto shape [I8], mass [I16], **de — ** in the form of a statue [I48]

buñuelo doughnut [II3]

burdo coarse [II23]

bureo secret meeting [II15]

buril chisel [II32]

burla joke [I3], **pesada —** biting jest [I21], **en —s** as a joke [I19], **de —** not seriously [I41]

burlado mocked[I27], tricked [II21]

burlador jokester [I52], deceiver [II48]

burlar to dally [I14], to joke [II9], to deceive [II48]; **—se** to play tricks [I19], to joke [I20]

burlería joke [II72]

burlesco, a lo in a parodying way [II22]

burlón jester [I4], joking [II62]

busca search [I20]

buscada search [I29]

buscar to look for [I4]

busilis secret [II45]

C

ca *arch.* for [I2]

cabal complete [I27], clever [II25]

cabalgadura mule [I29], mount [II40]

cabalgar to ride a horse [I29]

caballeresco chivalresque [prI]

caballería mount [I5], horsemen [II26], **— andante** knight-errantry [prI]

caballería(s) chivalry [prI], acts of chivalry [II8]

caballeriza stable [I2]

caballerizo groom [I21]

caballero knight [prI], gentleman

[I39], defensive construction from which one can fire guns [I39]; mounted (on horseback) [I7], riding along [II45]

caballerote big old gentleman [II5]

caballo horse [I1], **a** — on horseback [I8]

cabaña huts [I50]

cabecera head of bed [I36], head of table [I37]

cabellera lock of hair [II8]

cabello hair [I2]

caber to be contained [I21], to fall to one's share [I33], to fit [I37], to belong to [I39], —**le la suerte** to fall to one's lot [I4], — **en sí** to contain oneself [II62]

cabestro halter [I5], leading ox [II58]

cabeza head [I6], heading [II74], **de** — head first [I41]

cabial caviar [II54]

cabida influence [prI], favor [II42]

cabizbajo crestfallen [I22], with hanging head [I30]

cabo end [I2], stub [I3], cape [I41], place [II58], **al** — finally [I1], at the end [II23], **al** — **de** after [prI], **de** — **a cabo** from one end to the other [I16], **al cabo al** — in the long run [I8], **a** — after [I30]

cabra goat [I11]

cabrahigo wild fig tree [II22]

cabrerizo "goatish" [I20], goatherd [II41]

cabrero goatherd [I10]

cabrillas, las siete the Pleiades constellation [II41]

cabriola caper [II3]

cabrito baby goat, kid [I2]

cabrón he-goat [I2]

cachidiablo hobgoblin [I52]

cachorro lion cub [I46]

cacique Indian chief [II35]

cada each, — **cual** each one [I16], — **y cuando** provided that [I35], whenever [II31]

cadahalso = cadalso platform [II56]

cadáver body [II69]

cadena chain [I22]

cadenilla little chain [I32]

caer to fall [I37], to overlook [I40], to catch on [II7]; —**le mejor** to fit someone better [I7], — **de espaldas** to fall backwards [I24], — **en** to come to understand [I37]; — **en la cuenta** to realize [I49]

caída fall [I5], **dar una** — **abajo** to fall down [I16]

caída fall [II14]

caído fallen person [I19], fallen [I35], drooping [II14]

caja box [I6]

cajón typesetter [II62]

cala cove [I41], **— y cata**
   investigation [I6]
calabaza gourd [II66]
calabazada blow with head [I25]
calabozo jail [II11]
calabrés Calabrian [I40]
calado placed [II14]
calamidad misfortune [I15]
calamitoso calamitous [I9]
calandria lark [II19]
calar to understand [I47], to go
   down [II23], **—se** to close [I30],
   to lower oneself [II22]
caldera cauldron [II20]
calderada cauldronful [II13]
caldero cauldron [I11], pot [I35],
   bucket [II18]
calentar to give warmth [I24], to
   warm [II41]
calentura fever [I19]
caleta cove [I41]
caletre head [I23], brains [II3]
calidad rank [I3], nature [I29]
caliente hot [II47]
calificado worthy [II11]
caliginoso dark [II74]
callado reserved [I20], silent
   [II48]
callandico keeping quiet [II26]
callar to keep quiet [I7], to shut
   up [I22], to stop talking [I42]
calle street [I14], **hacer —** to clear
   a passage [II38]
callejuela narrow street [II38],
   sin salida cul-de-sac [II9]

callo corn on foot [II57]
caloña slander (archaism) [II2]
calumnia slander [II2]
calumniado slandered [II2]
caluniar to hold responsible [prI]
caluroso hot [I2]
calvatrueno crazy person [I52]
calza entera long pants [II43]
calzado footware [II51]
calzar to put on [I3], **—se** to put
   on shoes [I28]
calzas skirt [I1], **medias —**
   stockings [I22]
calzones pants [I20]
cama bed [I2]
cámara chamber [reI]
camarada friend [I40]
camaranchón garret [I16]
cambronera thorny bush [II22]
camello camel [II70]
caminante traveler [I13]
caminar to travel [I2]
camino journey [I2], road [I2], **en
   —** on the way [I42], **— real**
   highway [I15], **— de** towards
   [I4], along the way [I20], **abrir
   —** to find a way [I37]
camisa shirt [I3], nightshirt [I16]
campana bell [I22], **a — herida**
   souding the alarm [I22], in
   public [II6]
campanario belltower [I25]
campaña level country [I8],
   campaign [I22], open field
   [II17], **tienda de —** field tent

[II58]

campear to flourish [II1]

campeador warrrior [II33]

campo countryside [I2], field [prI], — **real** camp [I18], **en** — in the open air [I19], — **franco** open field [II56]

camuza chamois skin [II18]

can dog [I41]

cana white hair [I22]

canal channel [II29]

canalla rabble [I3]

canario canary [I22]

canasta basket [I22]

canción song [I12]

cancionero poetry collection [I6]

candado padlock [I51]

candayesco Candayan [II39]

candeal white wheat [I2]

candelero candlestick [II69]

candelilla little candle [II25]

candil oil lamp [I16]

candilazo blow with lamp [I17]

canequí muslin [II38]

canilla shinbone [II1]

canino canine [II20]

canísimo very white [II23]

cánones canon law [II19]

canonicato canonry [II13]

canónigo canon [I47]

canonizar to approve [I34], to beatify [II8]

cansado tired [I2]

cansancio weariness [I5], exhaustion [I19]

cansar to bother [I41], to tire [II63], **-se** to get tired [I4], to tire oneself [I6], to bother [II58]

cantar to sing [I5], to confess [I22]

cantarillo pitcher [I30]

cántaro pitcher [I20], **tener una alma como** — to be kind [II13], **alma de** — crazy person [II31]

cantía = cuantía importance [II41]

cantidad quantity [I7], **rata por** — prorated [II7]

cantillo pebble [I30]

cantimplora copper wine vessel [II45]

canto song [I8], stone [pról. II]

cantor singer [I22]

cantueso lavender, **flores de** — trivialities [II5]

caña reed [I2], — **de pescar** fishing rod [II13]

cañaheja tall pole [II45]

caño sewer [II22]

cañón cannon [I38], tube [II21], —**oñes** stubble [II41]

cañutillo, oro de gold thread [I31]

cañuto tupe [pról. II]

caos chaos [prI]

capa hiding place [I39], cape [II8], — **gascona** hooded cape [II26]

capataz field foreman [I28]

capaz spacious [I46]

capellán chaplain [aprob. II]

capellina hood [II4]
capellina helmet [II4], hood [II4]
caperuza cap [II45]
capilla chapel [dedI], hood [II42]
capirote hood [I52]
capital principal [I41], capital
   [II39]
capitán captain [prI]
capitana flagship [I39]
capítulo chapter [prI], provision
   [II20]
capón capon [II43]
capotillo cape [I28]
caprichoso capricious [I52]
captar to appeal to [II38]
captivo captive person [I36]
capuchino Capuchin monk [I11]
capullo de seda cocoon [II14]
capuz cloak [II23]
cara face [I12]
caracol snail
caramanchón garret [I36]
caráter character [II35]
carátula theater mask [II11]
carbón coal [I33]
carbunco carbuncle [I50]
carcaj quiver [II11]
carcaño heel [I17]
cárcel jail [prI]
carcoma grief [II8]
carcomer to eat away [II62]
carcomida eaten away [I52]
cardado carded [II14]
cardenal black and blue mark
   [I16]

cardinal cardinal [II18]
carecer to lack [prI], to miss [II60]
carestía scarcity [pról. II], want
   [II51]
carga load [prI], burden [I12]; —
   cerrada without looking [I6]
cargar to gather [I15], to weigh
   upon [I18], to load [I19], to
   burden [I22], — la mano to
   pursue eagerly [I29]
cargo charge [prI], position [I8],
   job, weight [I25], care [I33],
   burden [II51], claim [II74]; a —
   in charge [II44], a — de duty
   [I3], under the command of
   [I39]; tomar a su — to
   undertake[II1]
caricia caress [I42/43]
caridad charity [I27]
carirredondo round-faced [II10]
carísimo very dear [prI]
caritativo charitable [I12]
Carlo Magno Charlemagne [I49]
carmesí crimson [II21]
carmín scarlet [II48]
carnal first relative (as first
   cousin) [I5]
carnaza ham [II35]
carne flesh [I1], — y hueso flesh
   and blood [I18]
carnero lamb [I1], sheep [I18]
carnestolendas carnival [I17]
carnicería butcher stand [II51]
carnicero carnivore [II68]
caro dear [I42], lo — good wine

[II66]

carrera wandering [I2], course [I13], route [I45], running [II20], line [II35]; — **tirada** full gallop [I52], **de** — quickly [II23]

carreta cart [II11]

carretero cart driver [I10]

carril road [II33]

carrillo cheek [I20]

carrioche wagon [II11]

carriola small rolling bed [II70]

carro cart [I31]

carroza coach [II36]

carta card [II17], — **de pago** receipt [I25], — **misiva** personal letter [I23]

cartapacio notebook [I9]

cartel placard [II41]

cartero messenger [II67]

cartón cardboard [I1]

cartujo Carthusian [I13]

casa station [I39], — **de devoción** shrine [I8], — **de placer** country house [II30]

casaca coat [I41]

casada married women [II16]

casado married [I33]

casamentero matchmaker [II60]

casamiento marriage [I12]

casar to marry [II5], —**se** to get married [I12]

cascabel jingle bell [II11]

cascajo gravel [II5]

casco head [II2], —**s** brains [I31]

casero everyday [I41]

casi almost [prI]

casilla cottage [II2]

caso occasion [I2], chance [I9], event [I36], incident [I42], **puesto** — since [I13], **puesto** — **que** although [I3], **al** — to the purpose [I2], **hacer** — to pay attention [I3], **hacer al** — to do good [I7]

caspa dandruff [II44]

casta descent [II6]

castaño chestnut tree [I20]

castellano warden of castle [I2], Spanish [I8], Castilian [II62]

castigado chastised [I3]

castigar to punish [I16]

castigo punishment [I6]

Castilla Castile [reI]

castillo castle [I1]

castizo pure-blooded [I45]

casto chaste [prI]

castor beaver [I21]

castrador gelder [I2]

cata de, darse to suspect [I1]

catadura looks [I52], face [II70]

catálogo list [prI]

catar to examine, to look at [II71], —**se** to imagine onself [I21]

catarata cataract [II10]

catarro cold [II22]

catarse to expect [II1]

Catay China [I52]

cátedra professorship [II10]

catedrático professor [II4]

caterva multitude [prI]

católico Catholic [I47], good [II13], **no —** [I47] fishy [I47]

catorceno low-quality cloth, such as flannel [II5]

caudal wealth [II29]

caudaloso mighty [II67]

causa cause [I2], legal case [I22]l, case [II13]

causadora causer [I23]

causar to cause [I5], to cast a shadow [II32]

cautela, sin unscathed [I20]

cautivar to capture [I33], to captivate [II20]

cautiverio captivity [prI]

cautivo captive [I2], wretched [I4]

cauto wary [I8]

cava moat [I2]

cavar to dig [I13]

caverna cavern [II22]

caviloso distrustful [I40]

caya = caiga [I23]

cayado shepherd's hook [I12]

cayo = caigo [I34]

caza hunt [I1], game [II20]

cazador hunter [I21]

cazar to hunt [I33]

cazo ladle [II34]

cebada barley [I3]

cebar to excite passion [I33], to bait [II13]

cebo feed [aprob. II]

cebolla onion [I10]

cebollino Sancho's version of **cibelino** *sable* [II53]

cebolluda stuffed with onions [II48]

cebra zebra [I18]

Ceca en Meca, de from one place to another [I18]

cecina jerky [II49]

cédula permission [reI], order [I25], contract [II38], **— de recibo** receipt [I46]

cedulilla prescription [II71]

cegar to obscure [I18], to blind [I28]

ceguedad blindness [I16]

ceguezuelo little blind [II56]

ceja eyebrow [I13]

celada de encaje covered helmet [I1]

celar to conceal [I24]

celebérrimo most celebrated [prI]

celebrado venerated [I5], famous [I18]

celebrar to sing [I27], to praise [I50], **—se** to take place [II19], to greet [II44]

celebro = cerebro brain [I1]

celemín dry measure equal to a gallon [II50]

celeridad speed [I46]

celeste celestial [II8]

celestial celestial [II11]

celillo small jealousy [I20]

celo zeal [I11], **—s** jealousy [I6]

celos jealousy [I42/43]
celosía lattice [I40]
celoso jealous [I2], suspicious [I16]
celsitud loftiness [II30]
cena dinner [I3]; (= escena) scene [I48]
cenado eaten dinner [I11]
cenar to dine [I20]
cencerril pertaining to cowbells [II46]
cencerro cowbell noise [I23], bell [I46]
cencerruno bell-ish [II48]
cendal thin silk [I16]
cenizas ashes [I6]
censos, echar to invest [II13]
censurador censor [II3]
censurar disapprove of [II6]
centinela sentry
centro environment [II58]
ceñido tightly bound [I28]
ceñir to gird [I3], to bind [I27]
cepa grapevine [II2]
¡cepos quedos! careful! [II23]
ceptro scepter [II7]
cera wax [I25]
cerbatana ear trumpet [II62]
cerbelo brain [II22]
cerca = acerca about [I10]; — de near [I1], about [I4]
cercado surrounded [I38], walled [II45]
cercano near [II27]
cercar to surround [I39]

cercen a cercen from one end to the other [I35]
cercenar to cut off [II26]
cerco rim [II20]
cerda hog's bristle [I30], hair [II10], ganado de — pigs [I45]
cerdoso bristly; dealing with pigs [II68]
ceremonia formality [I11]
ceremonial book of ceremonies [I3]
cerimonia = ceremonia [I15]
cernadero thick cloth [II32]
cernícalo hawk [II43]
cernido sifted [I50], sifting [II32]
cerra *slang* hand [II57]
cerrado sealed [I13]
cerrado dense [I23], a puerta cerrada wholly [II74]
cerradura lock [I33]
cerrar to attack [I4], to follow [II65], — la noche to get dark [I3], —se to confine oneself [II44], — de golpe to slam shut [II44]
cerrera wanderer [I50]
cerro hill [II33], bragas de — pants made of hemp [II50]
cerrojo door latch [I42/43]
certeza certainty [I40]
certidumbre certainty [II1]
certificar to assure [I42], to certify [aprob. II]
cerviz nape of neck [I46]
cesado stopped [I22]

cesar to stop [I7]

cetro scepter [I13]

cevil = civil [I22]

chamelote de aguas wavy camel material [II44]

chamuscar to singe [II41]

chancillería chancery [priv. II]

chapa good sense [I25], plate [II67]

chapado spirited [II21]

chapín fine ladies' shoe [II5], — de la reina Queen's marriage tax [I45]

chapitel pinnacle *architectural term* [I2]

chata, nariz snub-nosed [II3]

chichón bump on head [I17]

chico small [II24]

chicoria = achicoria chicory [I8]

chillador town-crier [II26]

chimenea fireplace [I16]

china pebble [II49]

chinche bug [II12]

chinela slipper [II48]

chirimía double-reeded musical instrument [II26]

chirrio creaking [II34]

chocarrero coarse comic person [II49]

choquezuela joint [II53]

choza hovel [I2], hut [I10]

chufeta jibe [I31]

chupado sucked [II54]

churrillera charlatan [II45]

churumbela double-reeded instrument [II67]

chusma crowd [II23], crew [II63]

cibera wheat [I4]

cicatriz scar [I1]

ciceroniano Ciceronian [II32]

ciego blind [I34]; blind person [I50]

cielo heaven [prI], sky [prI]

ciencia science [I12]

cieno mud [I20]

ciento one hundred [I5]

cierto certain [I3], true [I1], for certain [I17]; **por** — indeed [I42]; **tener por** — to be certain [I19]

cifra emblem [I34], **en** — in effect [II38]

cifrado condensed [prI]

cifrar to enumerate [prI], to summarize [II63]

cigüeña stork [II12]

cima completion [I21], top [II8], **por** — **de** on top of [I14], **dar** — **a** to conclude happily [I44]

cimenterio cemetery [II9]

cimiento foundation [I52]

cimitarra scimitar [I35]

cincha girth [I4]

cinchado striped pig [II8]

cinchar to tighten [II10]

cínico cynical [aprob. II]

cinta ribbon [I2], belt [I46]

cinto belt [II73]

cintura waist [I8]

ciñese *past. subj. of* **ceñir** to gird

[I3]
ciñó girded *pret. of* ceñir [I3]
ciprés cypress [I13]
circuito surroundings [II60]
círculo circle [II9]
circunstancia detail [I27], incident [I41]
circunstante person present [I8]
circunvecino neighboring
cirial processional candle [I52]
cirujano surgeon [I25]
cita Scythian [I18]
citación references [prI]
citar to cite [prI]
ciudad city [I51]
ciudadano city dweller [I35]
civil, muerte death with loss of property [I22], wretched death [II39]
clara, a la plainly [I34]
claraboya skylight [II8]
claramente clearly [I17]
claridad clarity [prI], brightness [I3]
clarín bugle [I18]
clarísimo most illustrious [dedI]
claro clear [I6], bright [I20], illustrious [I32], de — directly [II72], de — en claro from sunset to sunrise [I1]
claustro cloister [I9]
clavar to stare [I23], to nail down [I46], to nail [I53]
clavija peg [I49]
clavo nail [II19]

clerical of the clergy [I23]
clérigo cleric [I12]
clima climate [I33]
cobarde coward [I4]
cobardía cowardice [I44]
cobijar to cover [II32]
cobrar to receive [I1], to recover [I3], to collect [I17]
cobre copper [II19]
cobro, en in hiding; poner en — to resolve [II53]
cocer to cook [I17], to bake [II25]
coche coach [I8]; — acá call use for swine
cochero cart driver [II11]
cocido cooked [I2], — o asado no matter what [II44]
cocinero cook [I10]
coco bogeyman [II74]
cocodrilo crocodile [II39]
codicia greed [I41]
codiciado much desired [II65]
codiciar to covet [I14]
codicilo codicil of will [II7]
codicioso greedy [I27]
codo elbow [prI], cubit [II1]
cofia hairnet [II44]
cofradía brotherhood [I21]
cofre jewel box [I35], chest [I26]
cofrecillo little trunk [I41]
coger to reap [I4], to take [I31], to gather [I41], to pick up [pról. II], to strike [II28], to catch [II42]
cogido caught [I49]

cogote back of the head [I16], back of neck [I26]

cohechar to bribe [II38]

cohecho bribe [II32]

cohete rocket [II41]

cohondir = confundir confound [I25]

coima *gypsy slang* concubine [I16]

cojear to limp [I5]

cojín saddle cushion [I23]

cojo lame [I21]

cola tail [I27], train [II37], **a —** at the rear [I52]

colada wash [I20]

colambre thirst [II54]

colar washed clothing [I22]

colcha quilt [I16]

colchado quilted [I27]

colchón mattress [I16]

colegio school [erratas I]

colegir to deduce [I2]

cólera rage [I4] bile [I6], **cortar la — ** to have a snack [I21]

colérico wrathful [I9], angry [I25]

coleto jacket [I23]

colgado in suspense [I8], hanging [I16]

colgar to hang [I26]

collar necklace [I29], collar [I45]

colmado filled [I49]

colmar to bestow [prI], to fulfill [I42], to fill up [I18]

colmena beehive [I28]

colmillo tusk [II34]

colmo abundantly full [I33], filled [I51]

colocado placed [prI]

colodra, de zoca en from one place to another [I18]

colodrillo back of head [I20]

coloquio conversation [I3]

color complexion [II2], **darle** to give it credence [I41]

colorado red [I35]

colorar to color [I40]

columbrar to see afar off [I21]

coluna column [II7], pillar [I10]

comarca region [I52]

combate combat [I19]

combatiente combatant [I9]

combatir to battle [I3]

comedia play [I25]

comediante theater director [I48]

comedidamente courteously [I2]

comedido polite [I22]

comedimiento politeness [I13], courtesy [II18]

comedor glutton [II59]

comento commentary [II3]

comenzado begun [I2], having begun [I32]

cometer to commit [I4]

comilón glutton [II2]

comisario deputy [I22]

comisión assignment [tasa II], commission [II44]

cómitre rower boss [II63]

como when [I2], as long as [I18],

since [I26], if [I37], — **que** as if
[I3]

cómo: el — ni el cuándo
explanation [II27], — **ni cómo**
no why [II42]

cómodamente comfortably [I41]

comodidad means [I27],
opportunity [I34],
accommodation [I34],
advantage [I36], **con —**
comfortably [II19]

cómodo dignity [I42], **tenga —**
be able [I31]

compadre friend [I6]

compaña = compañía company
[I10]

compañero companion [I2],
friend [I3]

compañía company [I51]

comparación comparison [I33]

comparar to compare [I1]

compás rhythm [I19], **a —**
rhythmic [I20], **— de pies**
fencing move [II19], **ir con el**
— en la mano to be prudent
[II33]

compasión pity [I32],
compassion [I42]

compasivo compassionate [I17],
doleful [I19]

compatriote,-to fellow
townsman [I29]

compeler to compel [II12]

compelido obliged [I33]

competencia debate [I1],
competition [II20]

competidor rival [I51]

competir con to rival [I6]

complacer to accommodate,
humor [I4]

complexión constitution [I1]

componer to write [I1], to restore
[I28], to arrange [II10], to
invent [II23], to make [II40], to
set type]II62], to compose
[II62], **—se** to be written [dedI],
to get ready [II21]

composición composition [I47]

compostura composure [I28],
made-up [I32], composition
[I50], demeanor [II11]

compra purchase [I9]

compuerta floodgate [II12]

compuesto mended [I2], written
[tasa I], fresh [I11], adorned
[I27], dressed up [I41], put
together [I51], compound
[II47], decorated [II51];
compound *n* [I17]

compungirse to be pierced with
remorse [II28]

cómputo computation [II29]

común public [I11], common
[I39]; town [I40]

comunicación communication
[II44]

comunicar to talk [II13], to
communicate [14], to consult
[I45], to give [I48], to
accompany [II62]

comúnmente commonly [prI]
comúnmente commonly [II16]
con que if [I24], so [I33], provided that [II28], — **todo eso** nevertheless [I22]
concavidad recess [II23], concavity *Sancho's mistake for* **cabida** *favor*[II33]
concebir to conceive [I11], to feel [I27], to imagine [I52]
conceder to concede [I7], to admit [I27], to allow [I29], to go along [II30]
concedido granted [I8]
concejil communal [II10]
concejo municipality [I40]
concepto *see* **conceto** [II16]
concepto literary conceit [II20]
concerniente concerning [I13]
concertado harmonized [I14], arranged [I21], orderly [I47], well-chosen [II1]
concertar to agree on a price [I20], to agree [I21], to accord [I24], to contrive [I33], to arrange [I46]
conceto = concepto literary conceit [prI]
concha shell [II6]
conciencia conscience [I10], mind [I49], **libertad de —** freedom of worship [II54]
concierto agreement [I9], arrangement [I41], harmony [I50]

concluir to finish [I3], to terminate [I1]
concluyente conclusive [I33]
concordar to agree [I39]
concordia harmony [I11]
condado county [I16]
condazo big old count [II5]
conde count [dedI]
condecender to submit [I27], to condescend [II49]
condenado condemned [I5], sentenced [I22], prisoner [I22]
condenar to condemn [dedI], to sentence [I22]
condesa countess [II5]
condesil, a lo as a countess [II5]
condición characteristics [I1], disposition [I1], rank [I14], tendency [I39], nature [I48], temperament [I50], danger [II48]; — **blanda** good temper [II24]
condolerse to feel sorry for [II70]
condolido sad [II29]
conducido led [I14]
conducir to lead [I12]
condumio ordinary food [II59]
condutor conveying [II25]
conejo rabbit [I50]
confesar to acknowledge [I4], to confess [I21], to concede [II28], —**se** t oconfess one's sins [II74]
confesión acknowledgment [I4]
confesor confessor [II43]
confiado confident [I4]

confianza confidence [I17]

confiar to trust [I33]; —**se** to fill with hope [I14]

confinante bordering [aprob. II]

confirmación confirmation [I27]

confirmado consumed [I9]

confirmar to declare [I29], —**se** to confirm (oneself) [I1]

confiscación confiscation [II60]

conflito struggle [I25]

conformar to conform [I14]

conforme a consistent with [I2], in accordance with [reI]

conformidad form [II16]

confortativo strengthening [II1]; tonic [II58]

confundir to master [prI], to confound [I41], to plunge [I52], to refute [II37]

confusión chaos [I41], confusion [I46], shame [II12]

confuso perplexed [I3], fearful [prI], confused [I48]

confutación disproof [prI]

congoja anguish [I17]

congojadísimo very distressed [I16]

congojado distressed [I17]

congojar = acongojar to distress [I10], —**se** to be distressed [I18]

congojoso distressed [II7]

conjetura conjecture [I52]

conjeturando speculating [I23]

conjeturar to conjecture [I17]

conjurar to implore [I24], to beseech [I48]

conjuro entreaty [II48]

conllevador fellow sufferer [II53]

conllevar to put up with [II13], to share [II68]

conmover to move [I39]

conmovido moved [I20]

conocer to recognize [I5], to learn [I42]

conocido known [I1], well-known [I2], acquaintance [I27]

conocimiento acquaintanceship [prI], knowledge [I33], recognizing [II11]

conquistado conquered [I15]

conquistar to overcome [I24], to win [II52]

consabidor accomplice [II49]

consagrarse to devote oneself [II20]

consecuencias, hacer to draw inferences [I49]

conseguir(se) to obtain [aprob. II]

conseja fable [I20], old wives' tale [I42]

consejero adviser [prI]

consejo advice [I3]; court [tasa I], —**s** advice [prII]

consentimiento consent [I28]

consentir to allow [I2], to permit [I3]

conserva compote [II51]

conservar to preserve [I6]

consideración contemplation

[I13], consideration [I48], thought [II59]

considerar to consider [I7]

consiguiente, por el (mesmo) consequently [I33]

consistir en to be comprised of [I2], to consist of [I3]

consolación consolation [I46]

consolar to console [I27], —se to be consoled [I21]

consorcio union [I46]

consorte companion [II30], spouse [II42]

constar to record, register [tasa I]

constituido made [II8], ordained [II32]

construir to construe grammatically [I40]

consuegro child's father in law [II47]

consuelo solace [I24]

consulta conference [II7]

consumadamente perfectly [I25]

consumado consummate [II18]

consumido tormented [II18], consumed [II21]

consumir to consume [I1]

contado instantly [I29]; **de —** on account [I25], in cash [II54]

contagio contagion [aprob. II]

contar to relate [prl], to tell [prl], to count [I18], —se to consider oneself [I30]

contemplar to contemplate [II20]

contender to fight [II64]

contendor adversary *arch.* [II14]

contener to contain [reI], to restrain [II2]; —se to be contained [dedI], to contain oneself [pról. II]

contenido aforesaid *jurid.* [II14]

contentar to gratify [I14], —se to be satisfied [I1]

contentísimo very pleased [I4]

contento mirth [I2], joy [prl], satisfaction [I6], happiness [II20], —s amusements [I33]

contesto woven [II8]

contestura structure [I42/43]

contienda fray [I8]

contina, a la continuously [I25]

continencia restraint [I51]

continente mien [I4], way [II34]

contingencia risk [I33]

contingente fortuitous [I26]

contingible possible [II24]

contino = **continuo** [I25], continuously [I33]

continuado continuous [II34]

continuamente constantly [I13]

continuar to keep visiting [I33]

continuo continuous [I1]

contoneo affected gait [II36]

contorno vicinity [prl], **de —** around [I31]

contra against [prl], towards [II20]

contradecir to oppose [I7]

contrahacer to falsify [I18]

contrahecho strange [I2], fake

[I46], pretend [II58]

contramina defensive tunnel filled with explosives [I38]

contrapeso weight [II20]

contrapuesto diverse [I33], opposite [II29], — **con** compared to [I37]

contrapunto harmony of words [I14]

contrario contrary [I15], opposite [I18], enemy [I35], obstacle [II1]

contrario contrary [I50], enemy [II22]

contraseño = **contraseña** countersign [II25]

contrastado opposed [I14]

contrastar to resist [I42/43]

contraste opposition [I15]

contravenir to counteract [prI], to violate [I17], to countermine [II49]

contrecho crippled [I16], counterfeit [I25], injured [II64]

contumaz obstinate [I23]

convenencia agreement on terms [II14]

convenible right [I1]

conveniente useful [I29], appropriate [II36]

convenir to suit [I1], to be good [I15], to concern [I33], to agree [I45]

convertirse en to change into [I13]

convidar to invite [I11]

conviene a saber to wit [II17]

convite banquet [II16], invitation [II24]

copa cup [I11]

copiar to copy [II62]

copiosísimo very large [I18]

copla verse [I12]

complear to write verses [II68]

coplero ballad singer [II67]

coplita little verse [II38]

copo snowflake [I18], ball (of cotton) [II14]

coraje anger [I8], courage [I38]

coral coral [II21]

corazón heart [I2]

corazoncillo little heart [II10]

corbacho whip [I22]

corbeta bucking [I20]

corchete constable [II49]

corcovado hunchback [I4]

corcovo buck [II10]

cordal wisdom tooth [I18]

cordel line [II29], cord [II53], rope [II63], whip [II71], **a hurta** — on the sly [II32]

cordelejo, dar to joke [I20]

cordellate, de ribbed [II19]

corderilla little lamb [II57]

cordero lamb [II20]

cordobán Cordovan leather [II13]

cordobés Cordovan [II10]

cordón cord [II41]

cordura prudence [I23]

corma, en la trapped [II30]

cormana first cousin [II39]

cormano, primo first cousin [II39]

cornado coin worth 1/6 of a maravedí [I17]

corneja crow [I14]

corneta bugle [II34]

coro: de — by heart [prI], **saber de —** to know by heart [I22]

corona crown [I12], tonsure [II52]

coronado crowned [I1]

coronar to crown [I7], to crowd [II31]

corónica chronicle [II26]

coronista *arch.* chronicler [I2]

coroza conical penitent's hat [II69]

corpezuelo bodice [II50]

corpiño bodice [I27]

corporal of the body [I37]

corral yard [I2]

correa strap [I3]

correcto corrected [erratas I]

corredizo easily untied [I20]

corredor fleet [I1]; corridor [II8], gallery [II46], runner [II61]; **— de oreja** stockbroker [I22], **— de lonja** exchange broker [I22]

corregir to temper [II27], to correct proofs [II62]

correo courier [I27], messengers [II10]

correoso grimy [I31]

correr to run, to be valid [I25], to rattle [I31], to offend [II27]; **—se** to be offended [I2], to be ashamed [I25]; **todo el —** full speed [I8], **a todo —** at full speed [I21], **— parejas** to compare [II32]

correspondencia relations [I33], appreciation [II35], other entrance [II55], trick [II62], home [II72]

corresponder to correspond [I14], to return a favor [I24]

corrida run [I13], **de —** all at once [I26]

corridica little run [II10]

corridísimo very crestfallen [I31]

corrido ashamed [I19], embarrassed [II21]

corriente flow [prI], flowing [I11], current [II23], valid [II26]

corrillo circle [I12], gossip group [I28]

corro group [II38]

corroborarse to strengthen [II34]

corsario pirate [I41]

corsario pirate [I38]

corso raid [I40]

cortado cut [pról. II]

cortador trenchant [I9]

cortapisas trimmings [II5]

cortar to cut (off) [prI], to cross [II29]

corte court [I21], capital [I42/43]

cortedad smallness [dedI], lack [II58]

cortes procession [II10]
cortés courteous [I23]
cortesana courtesan [I11]

cortesanía courtliness [II37]
cortesano courtier, courtly
   knight [I6], courteous [I6],
   sharp [I25]
cortesía compliment [I47],
   courtesy [I11]
cortesísimamente very
   courteously [I42]
cortesísimo very courteous [II8]
cortésmente courteously [I13]
corteza bark of tree [I11]
corto short [I9], scant [II5], — **de**
   vista short sighted [I49]; little
   [I12]; concise [I34]
corva knee [II29]
corvo arched [I11]
cosa anything [I2]
cosario = corsario pirate [I39]
coscorrón knocks on the head
   [II26]
cosecha harvest [I11]
coselete armor [I2]
coser to sew [I52], to stick [II17]
cosido stitched [I20]
cosilla little thing [II32]
cosmógrafo cosmographer [prI]
cosquear to limp [II4]
cosquillas tickling [II10],
   nonsense [II32], **no consiente**
   — will not put up with
   anything [II10]

costa coast [II1]
costa expense [reI], cost [I5],
   coast [I40], **a — de** at the
   expense of [I27], —**s** costs [I15],
   expenses [I25], **de —** additional
   [II51]
costal sack [I15]
costar to cost [reI]
costezuela slope [I18]
costilla rib [I4]
costo price [I35]
costoso costly [I35]
costumbre habit [I4], quality
   [I28], custom [II1]
costura seam [I23]
cotejar to compare [I45]
coto half a palm [I31]
cotonía cotton [II23]
cotufas "food" [I30], delicacies
   [II20]
coyunda yoke [II33], —**s**
   matrimonial union [I11]
coyuntura connection [I28],
   opportunity [I24], circumstance
   [I41]
coz kick [I1]
crecer to grow [I11]
crecido swollen [I17], important
   [II29], long [I51]
crédito reputation [prI], belief
   [II9], confidence [II31], **dar —**
   to believe [I37]
credo credo [I17]
crédulo, de gullible [II3]
creencia belief [I42/43]

creer to believe [I3]

creído confident [II2]

cría colt [II10]

criado,-a servant [I4]; created [I12], raised [I25]; **bien —** well-mannered [I1], **más bien —** more courteously [I17]

criador = creador creator [I10]

crianza breeding [II12], upbringing [II48]

criar to rear [I15], to raise [II58]

criatura creature [I8]

criba sieve [II59]

cribar to sift [I18], to riddle [II69]

crin mane of a horse [I16]

cristal glass [I33], crystal [I28]

cristalino crystal [II23]

cristalino transparent [I18]

cristel enema [II12]

cristiandad Christendom [I39], Christianity [pról. I]

cristianesco Christian [I40]

cristiano Christian [prI]

crucifijo crucifix [I40]

crudeza cruelty [II13]

crudo uncooked, cruel [II13]

cruel cruel [I27]

crueldad cruelty [I4]

crujía amidships [II62]

crujir clanking [I20]; to crack [I45], to rustle (as a cloth) [II1], to clang [II12], to gnash [II34]

cruz cross [I6], the sign of the cross [I8]

cruzado Portuguese gold coin [II63]; crossed [II69]

cruzar to cross [I50]

cuadra room [II31]

cuadrado square [I37], square-toed [II24]

cuadrar to fit [I19]

cuadrilla gang [I14], company [I45], group [II19]

cuadrillero officer [I16]

cuajada cottage cheese [II21]

cuajado churned up [I18]

cual = como [I23], **lo —, el —** which [reI], **—es** some [II39]

cuál which [I4], someone [I12], how [I16]

cualesquier any *pl.* [reI]

cualidad quality [II13]

cualificado approved [I35]

cualque some [II13]

cualquiera any [I2], anything [I2]

cuan as [I25]

cuán how [I3]

cuando if [I33], **de — en cuando** once in a while [I5], **cada y —** whenever [II31]

cuanto however much [I5]l, everything [I39], **—s** as many [I7]; **— más** moreover [prI], not to mention [I10], more so [I20], besides [I40; **todo —** everything [I18], **todos —s** everyone [I17], **en — a** insofar as [I31]

cuánto how much [I2], all the more [I2]; **en —** insofar as [I2]

cuaresma Lent [II5]

cuartal loaf of bread [I18]

cuartana intermittent fever [I42/43]

cuartel quarter sections [I18], **a —es** in shifts [I41]

cuartillo pint [II20], quarter of a **real**, 9 **maravedís** [II26]

cuarto fourth [I6], **—s** horse hoof affliction [I1], hind quarters [I29], apartment [I21], coin = 4 **maravedís** [I35]

cuasi almost [I23]

cuatralbo commodore [II62]

cuatrero cattle rustler [I22]

cuatrín old coin of little worth [II62]

cuatro, con el fourfold [II42]

cuba barrel [II7]

cubierta shelter [I13], cover [II10]

cubierto covered [I5]

cubrir to cover [I11]

cuchara spoon [II20]

cucharada spoonful [II22]

cucharón ladle [II20]

cuchilla blade [II3]

cuchillada knife slash [I1]

cuchillo knife [I41]

cudicia = codicia greediness [I20]

cuello neck [I3], collar [I37]

cuenta calculations [I29], narrative [I5], reckoning [I7], bead [I16], count [I16], care [II33] accounting [II57]; **—s** accountings [II3], **en — on**

account [I4], **de —** of importance [I25]; **hacer —** to plan to [I4], to depend on [II4], to pay attention to [II16], **hacer la —** to calculate [I4], **en esa —** in that case [I18], **dar — de** to take care of [II41], **dar[le] —** to give an account [I18], **tener —** to be careful, to take care of [I31], **hacer —** to realize [I31], **dar —** to reveal, tell [I35], **tener — con** to take care of [I31], **caer en la —** to see [I33], to realize [I49], **dar — de** tell [I33], **hacer — to** consider [I33], **entrar en — to** think [I50]

cuento story [I1], subject [I48], end [II14], **a —** opportune [I25], **no ponerse en —s** not try to vie [I5]

cuerda rope [I16], wick [I41]

cuerdo sane [I22], discreet [II43]

cuerno horn [I2]

cuero leather [I4]; **en —** naked [I22], skin [I35]

cueros, en naked [I25]

cuerpo body [prI], volume [I6], **—s** bodice [II36], **—s del rey** royalty [II22]

cuervo raven [I13]

cuesco stone *seed* [II70]

cuesta hill [I18], **a —s** on one's shoulders [prI], intact [I9], on one's back [I22]

cuestión matter (*see also*

quistión) [II19]

cueva cave [I23]

cuidado care [I2], worry [I42/43]

cuita affliction [I2]

cuitado unfortunate person [I21]; afflicted [I42/43]

cuitísima great affliction *nonsense word* [II38]

culebra snake [I50]

culpa offense [I30], blame [I4], failing [I51]; **dar —** to blame [I42/43]

culpado condemned [I14]

culpar to blame [I33]

cultivado cultivated [prI]

cultivar to cultivate [II12]

cumbre summit [I34]

cumplido fulfilled [I7], long [I35], finished [I42/43]

cumplimiento fulfillment [II14], politeness [II21]

cumplir to fulfill [reI], to honor [I26], to perform [I29], to need [I36], **— con** to discharge [I4], **— con su palabra** to keep one's word [II41]

cuna cradle [II30]

cundido spread [aprob. II]

cundir to spread [I25]

cuñada sister-in-law [I42]

cuñado brother-in-law [II69]

cupiese past subjunctive of **caber** [II1]

cupo fit (*from* **caber**) [I19]

cura priest [I1], cure [I46]

curadillo codfish [I2]

curado parish [I26]; treated with medicine [II47]

curar to heal [I1]; **— de** to take care of [I2]; **—se** to pay attention [I3], to cure oneself [I3], to worry about [I31]

curiosidad inquisitiveness [prI], care [II40], curiosity [II49]

curioso curious person [I33]; inquisitive [I8], strange [I8], neat [I23], quaint [I31], in the know [II21], meddlesome [II33], diligent [II43], high-quality [II51]

cursado accustomed [I8]

cursar to take courses [II18]

curso current [I18], course [II74], **—s** course of events [II41]

curtido hardened by weather [II73]

curva curve [II26]

cutir to match against [II40]

cuyo whose [I6]

cúyo whose [II26]

D

dacá *see* **paja**

dádiva gift [I28], bounty [II20]

dadivoso generous [I39]

dado allowed [I8]; die [I20], **— falso** loaded dice [II33]; **bien —** delivered [I25], well-deserved [II26]

Dador God [I25]; **dador** giver [II58]

daga dagger [I27]

dama lady [prI]

damasco damask fabric [I37]

damiselas young lady [II62]

danza dance [I5]

danzador dancer [II62]

danzar to dance [II48], formal dancing [II62]

dañado wicked [I27]

dañador offender [I6]; harmful [I49]

dañar to harm [I12]

daño hindrance [I4], damage [I6], harm [II17]

dañoso harmful [II46]

dar to whip [II9], to get caught [II58]; — **en** to hit upon [I1], to take to [I12], to fall [I40], to insist on [II8]; — **por** to consider [II16]; — **con** to throw [I8], to come upon [II9], — **tras** to pursue [I69]; —**se a** to devote oneself to [I1], to dedicate oneself [I3], **no** —**se manos** not to be able [I22]; — **fe** to attest [tasa I], — **a conocer** to become known [I3], — **agua** to water [I3], — **parte** to inform [I2]. —**es y tomares** debits and credits [II74]

dardo pike [I22]

daría = diría [I34]

dátil date *fruit* [II21]

datilado date-colored [I37]

de from [II74]

declaración affidavit [II72]

debido due [I30]

débil weak [I33]

debilitado weakened [I3]

decantado exalted [I13], moved [II29]

decantarse to lean towards [II51]

decencia dignity [I37]

decendencia = descendencia origin [I21]

decender = descender to descend [I40]

decendían = descendían [I22]

decendiente = descendiente descendent [I8]

decente honorable [II14]

deceplinante = disciplinante flagellant [I52]

dechado model [I47]

decir to mention [I32]; calling oneself [II18], to jibe [II34]

declaración telling [II26], deposition [II72]

declarado simple [II14]; translated [II39]

declarador narrator [II25]

declarar to make known [I1], to declare [I8], to exemplify [I20], to explain [I22]

declinación downward direction [II74]

declinar to come to a close [II68]

decorar to recite from memory

[I11]

decoro decorum [prI]

decreto decree [tasa II]

dedito little finger [II18]

dedo finger [I10], **atar bien el —** to be careful [II7]

defecto defect [I33]

defender to maintain [I4], to defend [I8], to hold [II2], to prevent [II54], **—se** to defend onself [I4]

defensa protection [I11], defense [I8]

defensivo defensive [II16]

defensor defender [I39]

defraudado deprived [I13]

defraudar to defraud [I29]

degollado person with throat cut [II43]

degollar to behead [I30]

dehesa pasture [I15]

deidad deity [I41]

dejar to abandon [I2], to let go [I17], to leave [I26], to let [II9]; **— caer** to drop [I40], **— de** to fail to [prI], to stop [I12], **no — de** not to help but [I1], not to fail to [I1]

delante in front [I16]

delantera front [II17]

delantero in front [I20]

deleitable delightful [I42/43]

deleitar to delight [I11]

deleite pleasure [I24]

deleitoso delightful [II23]

delgadísimo very fine [I50]

delgado fine [I6]

deliberado considered [I13]

delicadeza fine point [I47]

delicado faint [I4], sensitive [I5], exquisite [I28], delicate [I33]

delincuente criminal [I22]

delinear to describe [II1]

deliñado, mal incapable of writing well [II74]

delito crime [I10]

demanda enterprise [I23], request [I24], challenge [I44], quest [I49], question [II23]

demandante plaintiff [II45]

demandar to want [II41]

demás = **además** besides, **lo —** the rest [I2], **los/las —** the others [I1], the remaining [I7], **a — quite** [II3]

demasía insolence [I3], excess [I17], odds [II4], **en —** in excess [I20]

demasiadamente overly [I7]

demasiado excessive [I6]

demonio devil [I33]

demostración demonstration [II20], **—ciones** behavior [I28]

demostrar to demonstrate [I2]

denantes = **antes** [II12]

denostar to revile [I19]

dentellear to gnash teeth [I19]

dentro inside [I6], **de —** inside [I1]

denuedo daring [I3], courage

[II14]

denuesto insult [I17]

denunciar to denounce [priv. II]

deparar to provide [prI], to present [I13], to come into sight [I15], —**se** to present oneself [I8]

departir to speak [I21]

deponer to lay aside [II1]

depositado placed in a cemetery vault [I19]

depositar to deposit [I6]

depositario depository [I13]

depósito storehouse [I9]

depravado depraved [II1]

deprecación prayer [II22]

deputado limited [I22]

derechamente properly [I48], directly [II27]

derechas, a correctly [I18]

derecho straight [I4], right [I17], fee [II51], **hecho y —** full-fledged [I18]; —**s** directly [I41], fees [II17]

derivar to trace [origins] [I21]

derramar to shed [I28], to spill [I35]

derredor: al — de around [II61]

derrengado battered [II14]

derretir to melt

derribado torn down [I3], flattened [I16], thrown [I11]

derribar to knock down [I1], to knock off [II19], to demolish [prI], —**se** to lower oneself

[II12]

derrota path [I7], road [I29], course [I41]

derrumbadero precipice [I28]

derrumbar to precipitate [I20]

desabridamente sourly [I33]

desabrido dissatisfied [I33], bad-tasting [II23]

desabrimientos worries [II74]

desabrochar to unfasten [I27]

desaconsejar to advise against [I12]

desacreditar to contradict [II43]

desafiar to challenge [I11]

desafío challenge [I1]

desaforado huge [I5], outrageous [I26]

desagradar to displease [I25]

desagradecido ungrateful [I12]

desagradecimiento ingratitude [II4]

desaguarse to drain [II48]

desaguisado injury [I2], outrage [I26]

desairado clumsy [II62]

desalentado discouraged [II59], sluggish [II68]

desaliñando having taken off the packsaddle [II12]

desalmado soulless [I5], wicked [II48]

desalumbradamente erroneously [aprob. II]

desalumbrado unenlightened [II62]

desamor indifference [I14]
desamodao unloved [II67]
desamparar to abandon [I3]
desamparo abandonment [II29]
desaparecer to disappear [I37], to make disappear [I51]
desapercebido unprepared [II1]
desarmar to remove armor [I2]
desarraigar to remove [II37]
desasirse to get loose [I16]
desasosegado restlessly [II44]
desasosegar to disturb [I20]
desasosiego anxiety [I24], disturbance [I45]
desastrado tattered [I28], disastrous [I42/43]
desastre disaster [I28]
desatacarse to take off pants [II60]
desatar to untie [I4], to let loose [I22]
desatentado disturbed [II21]
desatinado reckless [I35]
desatinar to go crazy [I25], to bewilder [I42]
desatino folly [I1]
desavenido on bad terms [II16]
desayunarse to break one's fast [I2], to take breakfast [I8]
desbaratado routed [I19], dissipated [II19], ill-advised [II49]
desbaratar to rout [I19]
desbastar to trim away [II42]
desbocado broken-lipped [II25]

desbuchar to disgorge [II2]
descabalado out of your mind [II23]
descabezar to behead [I25]
descaecimiento despondency [II1] low spirits [II11]
descalabrado wounded on the head [I17]
descalabrar to injure one's head [II13]
descalzarse to take off (stockings) [II44]
descalzo barefoot [I16]
descaminado gone astray [I14]
descansado with ease [I15], rested [I20]
descansar to rest [I46]
descanso repose [I2], rest [I37]
descargar to strike [I9], —**se** to clear oneself [II47], — **nublado** to vent one's anger [I31]
descargo relief [I48], unburdening [II29]
descarnada fleshless one [II20]
descarnado fleshless [II35]
descarnarse to lose weight [II66]
desceñido without a belt [II43]
desceñirse to take off [I18]
descoger to loosen [I28]
descolgar to take down [I29], to let down [II23], —**se** to let oneself down [I35]
descollarse to stand up [II35]
descolorido pale [I36]
descomedido rude [I1]

descomedimiento rudeness [II11]

descompostura slovenliness [II43]

descompuesto disarranged, disturbed [I28], brazen [II51], carefree [II62]

descomulgado excommunicated [I5]

descomulgar to excommunicate [I19]

descomunal huge [I1], monstrous [I4]

descomunión excommunication [I30]

desconcertado wild [I34]

desconcertar to disconcert [I14]

desconfianza jealousy [I23], mistrust [I14]

desconocido strange [I14], unfeeling [I42]

desconsolado grief stricken [I9]

descontar to deduct [I4]

descontentar to displease [I31]

descontento unhappy; unhappiness [I33]

descorazonado spirtless [II41]

descortés ill-bred [I4]

descortesía rudeness [I41]

descoser unsew [I46], —se to let loose one's tongue [II48]

descosido tattered [II14]

descrédito disrepute [II16]

descreer to disbelieve [I28]

descriarse to damage oneself

[II36]

describir to describe [I16], to see [I41]

descubierto found out [I21], hatless [I23], bare [I41], open [II11]; **al —** openly, **lo — del mundo** the known world [I21]; **al —** uncovered [I12]

descubridor discoverer [II25]

descubrir to discover [I4], to uncover [I2], to find [I2], to reveal [I12], to denounce [I40]; **— tierra** to find out [II28], to tell the truth [I24], to be seen [I41], **—se** to reveal oneself [I2]

descuidado careless [I4], unaware [I34], off guard [I41]

descuidar to not worry [I29], **—se de** to forget [I22]

descuido carelessness [I4], **en —** without cares [II60]

desculparse = disculparse

desde from [I41], **— luego** right now [I11], **— lejos** from afar [I3]

desdecir to differ [I1], to be unworthy [II12]

desdén scorn [I12]

desdeñado scorned [I20]

desdeñar to scorn [dedI]

desdeñosa disdainful [I14]

desdicha misfortune [I6]

desdichadísimo very unfortunate [II38]

desdichado unfortunate [I9],

wretched [I18]

desechar to reject [I23], to put aside [I29]

desembanastar to release an animal [II17]

desembarazadamente freely [II60]

desembarazado unencumbered [I22], open [I30]

desembarazar to unencumber [I3], — **el pecho** to clear one's throat [II12]

desembarcadero landing place [I20]

desembarcar to land [I30], to disembark [I41]

desembaular to disclose [II38]

desembolsar to disburse [I4]

desemejable incomparable [I20]

desenalbardar to remove the packsaddle [I25]

desenamorado out of love [II59]

desencajado wild (eyes) [II10]

desencajar to disconnect [I28], to open [II21], —**se** to fall apart [II20]

desencantar to disenchant [I21]

desencanto disenchantment [II35]

desencintar to take off a belt [II60]

desenclavijar to loosen the grip [I45]

desenfadadamente without embarrassment [I12]

desenfadado carefree [I25], self-confident [II43]

desenfado ease [I22]

desengañado rejected [I12]

desengañar to disabuse [prI], to learn the truth [I22]

desengaño reproof [I12], truth [I36] discouragement [I14], sanity [II29], —**s** sad teachings from experience [I6]

desenjaular let out of cage [I49]

desenlazar to unlace [II56]

desenredar to get free [II30]

desensillado unsaddled [II58]

desenterrar to dig up [II37]

desentonado humble [I23]

desenvainado unsheathed [I34]

desenvainar to release [II17], to unsheath [II21], to take out [II66]

desenvoltura poise [I3], boldness [I11], shameless act [I33], brazenness [I51]

desenvolver to unwrap [II48]

desenvueltamente in a free and easy way [I34]

desenvuelto free and easy [II48]

deseo desire [I2]

deseoso desirous [I9]

deservicio disservice [I27]

desesperado hopeless [I13], desperate [I25], despairing [I35]

desesperarse to despair [I2]

desfacedor *arch.* undoer [I4]

desfacer = deshacer [I19]
desfalcar to take [II71]
desfallecer to fail [I3]
desfavorecer to not do anything for [I50]
desfavorecido injured [I12]
desfigurado disfigured [I26]
desfigurar to deface [II26], to disfigure [II48]
desflorar to lose shine [II58]
desgajar to tear off a branch [I8]
desgarrado torn [II34]
desgarrarse to escape [II6]
desgobernado without a government [II4], ungoverned [II36]
desgracia misfortune [I3], enmity [I27]
desgraciado unlucky [I15], surly [II10]
desgreñado with uncombed hair [II50]
deshacedor undoer [I4]
deshacer to undo [I3], to right [I2], to redress [I1], to destroy [prI], to dissolve [I35]; —se de to get rid of [I39], to disappear [II4]
deshechar to scorn [II42]
deshecho destroyed [I4], in pieces [I23]
desheredado disinherited [I37]
deshogar to give vent to [I42/43]
deshonestidad lewdness [I34], indecency [I34]

deshonesto lustful [I34], immodest [I51]
deshonra disgrace [I15], dishonor [I48]
deshonrado disgraced [I28]
deshonrar to insult [I31]
deshora(s), a unexpectedly [prI], inopportunely [I20]
desierto wilderness [I3]; deserted [I41]
designio intention [I11]
designo = designio = plan [II7]
desigual dissimilar [I2], unequal [I8], arduous [II14]
desigualdad difference [I28]
desinteresado unsuspecting [I33]
desistir to give up [I20]
desjarretar to weaken [II7]
desleal disloyal [I5]
desleído liquid [I31]
deslenguado insolent [II60]
desliar to untie [II22]
desligar to untie [I20]
deslindar to clear up [I21], to survey [I22],
deslizar to slide [II12], —se to slip [II18]
deslocado dislocated [II64]
deslumbrar to dazzle [II65]
desmán misfortune [I23]
desmandado random [I38]
desmandarse to behave badly [II16]
desmantelar to tear down [I40]
desmayado faint [I18], dull [II43]

desmayar to diminish [I33]; —**se** to faint [I21], to droop [I48], to become weak [II65]

desmayo dismay [I9], swooning [I24], fainting spell [I27]

desmazalado weak [II43], dejected [II45]

desmedrado impaired [I27]

desmentir to contradict [I11], to deny [I22]

desmenuzado to cut to bits [II26]

desmesurado inordinate [II1]

desmochado cut off [I11]

desmoronar to dig out [II55]

desnarigado un-nosed [II14]

desnatar to skim off [II62]

desnudar to undress [I8], to strip [II29]

desnudez nakedness [I23]

desnudo naked [I4], plain [prI], lacking [dedI]

desobligar to release [I51]

desocupado idle [prI], unoccupied [I42]

desolado devastated [II26]

desollar to flay [I4], to skin [II2]

desoluto *rustic corruption of* **absoluto** [I12]

desordenado disordered [I50]

desorejar to cut the ear off [I40]

despabilar to eat up [II20], to solve [II51], — **los ojos** to open one's eyes [II10], —**se** to wake up [II33]

despachado dismissed [I27]

despachar to heed business [II49], to dispatch [II51]

despacho speed [I44], dispatch [II47]

despacio slowly [I2]

despaldado dislocated [I8]

desparcir to spread [I28]

despartir to stop [I35]

despavorido aghast [I34], terrified [I50]

despeado footsore [II73]

despechado despairing [I33]

despecharse to get angry [I46]

despecho dismay [I16], disrespect [I30], resentment [I40], **a — de** in spite of [I10]

despedida farewell [II4]

despedimiento farewell [II30]

despedir to dismiss [I2], to emit [I11], to throw [II11], to take leave [II26], —**se de** to say goodby [I7]

despedir to emit [II34], to fire [II48], —**se** to say goodby [II60]

despegador un-sticker [II13]

despejar to clear away [I33]

despensa pantry [I19], provisions [I23], —**s** provisions [II59]

despensero provider [II33], steward [II59]

despeñadero dangerous undertaking [I13]

despeñarse to dash [I20], to fall down precipitously [I20], to fling down [I27]

desperezarse to stretch oneself [II22]

despertador awakener [I20]

despertar to awaken [I8]

despiadado cruel [I4]

despierto awake [I7]

desplegar to spread [I20], to open [II10]

despoblado unpopulated area [I8]

despojar to rid [I14], to despoil [I21]

despojo spoils [I6]

despolvorear to clean [II17], —se to dust each other off [II14]

desposado groom [I27], —s bride and groom [II21]

desposarse to get married [II21]

desposorio marriage [I27], —s marriage vows [II21]

despotricar to rant [I25]

despreciar to scorn [prI], to ignore [II48]

desprecio contempt [I34]

después: — de after [I1], **— acá** since then [I27]

despuntar to dull [II58]

despuntar to manifest [I25]

destajar to cut [cards] [II7]

destemplado unharmonious [II36]

destemplanza abuse [II62]

desterrar to banish [I50], —se to banish oneself [I29]

destetar to be weaned [I48]

destierro exile [I6]

destilar to distill [II14]

destino fate [I14]

destraer = distraer to delude [II2]

destraído = distraído astray [prI], licentious [I2]

destreza skill [I10]

destripaterrones clodhopper [II5]

destroncar to cut off [I9]

destrozar to smash [I52]

destrozo destruction [II26]

destruición destruction [I30]

destruir to ruin [I27], to destroy [I41]

desuellacaras shameless fellow [I34]

desuncir to unyoke [I49]

desusado unusual [I36]

desválido destitute [I42/43]

desválido needy [I52]

desvalijar to rob [I19]

desvanecerse to faint [II41]

desvanecido smug [I48], vain [II44]

desvanecimiento fainting [II44]

desvariado extravagant [I13], nonsensical [II7]

desvariar to talk nonsense [II12]

desvarío delirium [I14]

desvelado awake [II48]

desvelar to keep awake [II60], —se to stay awake [I1]

desventura misfortune [I5]

desventurado unfortunate [I5]

desvergonzado shameless [II45]

desvergüenza impudence [I28]

desviado turned aside [I8], to one side [I42]; — **de** from [I41], away from [II43]; at variance with [II8]

desviar to get out of the way [I8], to move to one side [I42/43], —**se** to turn away from [I20], go away [II68]

desvío indifference [I11]

detener to check [I2], to detain [I22], to stop [I33]; — **el paso** to slow down [II19]; —**se** to stop [I14], to stay away [I21], to delay [I41], to pause [II27]

determinación resolution [I2], resolve [I17], decision [II21]

determinado determined [I27], fixed [II19], **lo** — resolve [I47]

determinar to conclude [prI], to determine [I6], to resolve [I24], —**se** to decide [dedI]

detestable loathsome [I11]

deuda debt [I2], indebtedness [I27]

deudor debtor [II45]

devaneo mad pursuit [I7], silly things [I32]

devengar to have an income [I21]

devoción devotion [I8], **casa de** — shrine [I8]

devoto devout [I3], holy [I52]

dezmar to reduce drastically [I33]

día daylight [II69], **otro** — the next day [I5], **en** —**s** old [I48]

diablo devil [I5], —**s** "the devil" [I35]

diabólico diabolic [I38]

diamante diamond [I18]

diamantino rigidly firm [I52]

dibujos, meterse en not to beat around the bush [II5]

dicha happiness [I23], good luck [II42], **a/por** — by chance [I2]

dicho named [prI], saying [prI]; aforementioned [reI], fortunate [I2], mentioned [I5]

dichoso fortunate [I4], happy [I40]

diciplina scourge [I52]; whipping [II35]

diciplinante = disciplinante flagellant [I52], penitent [II35]

diciplinarse to whip oneself [II68]

dictar to dictate [I29]

diente tooth [I13], **hablar entre** —**s** to mutter [I3], **dar** — **con diente** to chatter one's teeth [I19], **a** — fasting [I21], **entre mis** —**s** under my breath [I22]

diestra *arch.* right [I4]

diestramente skillfully [II21]

diestro skillful [II10], swordsman [I19]

dieta diet [II51]

dificultad obstacle [prI], difficulty [II50]

dificultar to make difficult [II3]
dificultoso difficult [I9]
difinición resolution [I45]
difinitivo absolute [I45]
difunto dead person [I12]; dead [I34]
digestión digestion [II47]
dignarse to condescend [II7]
dignidad office [I26]
dignísimo very worthy [II50]
digno worthy [erratas I]
digresión digression [II18]
dije trinket [I11]
dilación delay [II31]
dilatado long [pról. II], vast [II20], prolonged [II39]
dilatar to put off [I12], to delay [I36], to extend [II49], to delay [II63], —se to spread [I13]
dilicado = delicado delicate [II38]
diligencia diligence [I37], requirement [reI], device [I12], speed [I13], industry [I27], step [I41]; —(s) precaution(s) [I20], clever things [I28], preparations [II38]
diligente speedy [I47], busy [II20], assiduous [I32]
dime "dispute" [II26]
diminuir to diminish [I41]
Dinamarca Denmark [I10]
dinerillo bit of money [II52]
dinero money [I3], coin [II20]
Dios God [prI]

diosa goddess [I16]
diputar to deem [I1], to designate [I6]
dirétes "dispute" [II26]
dirigir dedicate [II24]
discantar to differ [II59]
discernir to discern [II34]
discorde dissonant [I27]
discordia discord [I45]
disciplinante penitent [I52]
discreción cleverness [prI], sagacity [prI], discretion [I3], acuteness of mind [I14], -es shrewd remarks [I24]
discretísimo very discreet [II38]
discreto ingenious, circumspect [I13], witty [I4], prudent [I11], shrewd [I20]; sharp person [prI]
disculpa excuse [I27]
disculpar to exculpate [I27], to apologize [I3], —se to apologize [I8]
discurriendo rambling [I18]
discurrimiento discussion [II59]
discurrir to discourse [I30], to roam [I33], to mull over [II27]
discurso thought [prI], speech [I1], course [I8], reasoning [I13], conjecture [I40], movement [I45], intention [I49], meditation [II63], **haciendo** — reasoning [II21]
disfigurado = desfigurado disfigured [I23]

disformimísimo very deformed
disfraz disguise [I27]
disfrazado disguised [I28]
disfrazar to disguise [I29]
disgustar to bore [II27]
disgusto vexation [I9]
disignio = designio thought [I21], intention [I37]
disimulación pretending [II17]
disimuladamente furtively [I41]
disimular to overlook [prI], to hide [I9], to dissemble [I20]
disminuir to lessen [II2]
disoluble undissolvable [I27]
disonar to not be in accord with [aprob. II]
disparar to discharge [prI], to fire a gun [I22], to hurl [II1], to shoot [I10], to blunder [II43]
disparatado absurd [I6], silly [I6]; foolish person [I51]
disparate nonsense [prI], extravagance [I22], blunder [I24]
dispensación dispensation [I29]
disponer to command [I1], to regulate [reI], to prepare [I33], to order [I45], to dispose of [I51], to take care of [II42], — **de** to have the use of [II69], —**se** to prepare oneself [I33], —**se a** to get ready [I7]
disposición trappings [II14], elegance [II41], will [II74]
dispuesto disposed [II13], **mal —**

indisposed [I21]
dispusición = disposición disposition [I28]
disputa dispute [II23]
disputar to question [II43], to dispute [II50]
distar to be distant [I38]
dístico couplet [prI]
distilado = destilado filtered [I50]
distintamente distinctly [I36]
distinto instinct [I21]
distributivo distributive [I37]
distrito district [II32]
disuadir to dissuade [I47]
ditado title [I37]
diversidad diversity [I33]
diverso different [I3]
divertido different [II34]
divertimiento diversion [approb. II]
divertir to amuse [I18], to divert [I24], to take one's mind off [I48], —**se** to wander [II38]
dividido separated [I22], divided [II14]
dividir to divide [I4], to separate [I27], —**se** to divide [I14]
divina escritura holy scripture [prI]
divinamente divinely [I1]
divinidad divinity [I1]
divino divine [prI], sacred [I48]
divisar to perceive [I4]
Divulgarse to make well-known

[II48]

do, dó = donde where [I14]

dobla doubloon = 212 **maravedís** [I41]

doblado bent double [I20]

doblar to go around [I20], to fold [I27], to double [I34], to bend [I40]; **—se** to yield [I34], to submit [I33]

doblegar to acquiesce [II35]

doblón gold coin worth as much as 8 **escudos** [II13]

docena dozen [II1]

docientos two hundred [II7]

docto learned [I1]

doctrina instruction [II38], **niño de la —** orphan [II35]

doctrinar to instruct [II42]

documento instruction [II42]

dogmatizador founder [I6]

dolencia pain [I27]

doler to feel for [I5], to hurt [I8], **—se de** to take pity on self [I49]

doliente sorrowful [I14]

dolo fraud [II3]

dolor pain [I8]

dolorido doleful [I14]

doloroso sorrowful [I26]

domeñar to tame [II12], to condescend [I21]

domingo Sunday [I52]

dominio control [I39]

don boon [I3], gift [II58]; **ponerse — to be called don** [I3]

donación gift [I17]

donaire grace [I2], witticism [prI]

donairoso witty [II30]

doncella maiden [I2], damsel [I27], when unmarried [II21]

doncellez virginity [II41]

donde when [I41], **— no** if not [I27]

dondequiera anywhere [I3], wherever [I36]

donoso witty [I6]

doquiera: a — wherever [I16], **por —** everywhere [I25]

dorado golden [I2]

dormido slept [I7], asleep [I7], sleepy [II35]

dormir sleep [I1], sleeping [I2], to calm [I20]

dormitar to doze [II12]

dornajo small trough [I11]

dos, entrambos a both [I33]

dosel curtain [II33]

dotado endowed [I49]

dotar to endow [II25]

dote dowry [I31], quality [II58]

doto = docto learned [I48

dromedario dromedary [I8]

ducado ducat [I22]

ducal of a duke [I21]

duda doubt [I14], **sin —** doubtless [I1]

dudar to doubt [I2]

dudoso perilous [I9], unreliable [I18], uncertain [I45], truthfulness [I47]

duecho = **ducho** accustomed [I7]

duelo duel [I15], sorrow [I18]

duende elf [II37]

dueña lady (in waiting) [I13]

dueñesco dueña-ish [II37], pertaining to a dueña [II38]

dueño owner [I4], master [II13]

dulce sweet [I1], delightful [aprob. II]

dulcísimo very sweet [I11]

dulzaina ancient double-reeded wind instrument [II26]

dulzura pleasure [I28]

duque duke [dedI]

duquesa duchess 3esca[II30]

dura vintage [II13]

durable lasting [I18]

duradero lasting [I25]

durar to last [I18]

dureza stiffness [I6], hardness [I16]

durísimo very hard [II58]

durmiendo asleep [I35]

duro hard [I2]

duro hard [I11], **a duras penas** with great difficulty [I21]

E

e *arch.* and [I4]

ébano ebony [II70]

eceptar = **exceptuar** to except [I15]

eceto = **excepto** [I3]

ecetuar = **exceptuar** to except [I6]

echacuervos charlatan [II31]

echado lying [II17]

echar to give to drink [I2], to throw out [I6], to put [I6], to bestow [II10], try out [II50], — **suertes** to draw straws [I12], — **mano** to take [I15], — **menos** to miss [I17]; —**se** to throw oneself [I21], — **a perder** to bring to ruin [I5], — **a rodar** to cast aside [I16], — **de ver** to notice [I4], — **a pechos**, take a drink [I17], — **de ver** to discover [I18], — **cata** to find out [II50], —**se a dormir** to go to sleep [II59]

eclesiástico of the Church [I29]; priest [II31]

écloga = **égloga** eclogue [II74]

eco echo [I14]

edad age [I1]

edificio memorial [I34], plot [II70]

efectivo permanent [II50]

efecto purpose [I25]; **en** — indeed [I7]

efeto = **efecto** purpose [reI], effect [I7]

efetuar to do [I44], —**se** to be realized [I27]

eficacia efficiency [II69]

eficacísimo very powerful

eficaz powerful [I34]

efigie effigy [II14]

efusión de sangre bloodshed

[I45]

égloga eclogue [I6]

ejecución execution [I22], **poner en —** to carry out [I13]

ejecutar to perform [I4], to carry out [II54]

ejemplar exemplary [pról. II]

ejemplo example [I34]

ejercer to practice [I22]

ejercicio profession [I1], practice [I1], activity [I28]

ejercitar(se) to put into practice [I1], to practice [I37]

ejército army [I18]

elección choice [I14]

eleción = elección choice [I18]

electo appointed [II32]

elefante elephant [II12]

elegante elegant [I48]

elegantemente elegantly [II49]

elevado absorbed [II34]

elevamiento rapture [prI]

Elíseos, campos Elysian Fields [I13]

ello that [II69]

elocución elocution [I48], good style [II62]

elocuencia eloquence [I48]

elocuente eloquent [I47]

elogio eulogy [prI], praise [aprob. II]

embaído deceived [I48]

embaidora deceiver [II45]

embajada message [I20]

embajador messenger [II50]

embarazar to hinder [II45], to encumber [II14]

embarazo impediment [I4]

embarazoso encumbering [I41]

embarcadero departure port [II24]

embarcar to embark [II60]

embarcar to ship [I31], to embark [I39], to take on board [I40]

embasar to get [II50]

embaular to stow away [I11], to throw in [II49]

embazar to hesitate [I44]

embebecido bemused [I12]

embeber to suppress [II4], to swallow up [I10]

embebido immersed [II2]

embelecador deceiving [II3]

embeleco deceit [II16]

embelesado spellbound [I28], stunned [II53]

embelesamiento spell [I23], reverie [II11]

embestir to assail [I8], to attack [I18], to crash [I41], to seize [I3]

embobado gaping [I11], fascinated [I32]

embocar to enter [II29]

emboscarse to retreat to a forest [I22]

embotar to blunt [I18]

embozado veiled [I36]

embozarse to cover one's face [I34]

embozo mask [I36]

embrazar to clasp [I2]

embuste trick [I6], scheme [II13]

embustero imposter, trickster [I22]

embutirse to hide [II11]

emendar = **enmendar** to correct [I2]

emienda = **enmienda** emendation [I6], improvement [I12], **hacer la** — to make amends [I19]

eminente eminent [I38]

empachado awkward [II7]

empachar to be reluctant [I30]

empacho obstacle [I47], bashfulness [II63]

empalar to impale [I40]

empanada meat pie [I50]

empañarse to fog [I33]

empapado saturated [I18]

emparedado confined [II53]

empecer to hinder [II32]

empedernido hard-hearted [II46]

empedrado set (as stones in jewelry) [II21]

empedrar to mix with° [II50]

empeñado pawned [I22]

empeñar to pawn [I7], to engage in [I16]

emperador emperor [I11]

emperante emperor [I5]

emperatriz empress [I4]

empero however [I27]

empinado standing up [II58]

empinar to raise [I8]

emplastado covered with plasters [I17]

emplastar to apply plasters [I16]

emplasto plaster [I15]

empleadísimo spent [II24]

empleado invested [I2], **mal** — wasted [II25]

empobrecer to become poor [II48]

empós de = **en pos de** in pursuit of [I12]

empozarse to engulf oneself [II22]

emprender to undertake [I20]

emprenta = **imprenta** print shop [pról. II]

empreñarse to get pregnant [II25]

empresa undertaking [I2], device or motto [I2]

emprincipio beginning [II7]

empujar to impel [I37]

empujón push [II74]

empuñadura hilt [II19]

empuñar to grasp [I52]

émula emulator [I9]

émulo rival [I45]

en at [I31], — **hora maza** = **enhoramala** blazes! [I5]

enajenado transferred [I29]

enalbardado with a packsaddle [II20]

enalbardar to saddle a donkey [I13]

enamorado in love [I1]; lover

[prI]

enamorar to cause love [I14], —se to love [I1]

enano dwarf [I2]

enarbolar to raise high [I16], to brandish [I52]

enarcar to arch [I23]

Enares = **Henares** a Spanish river [I6]

encadenado chained [I45]

encajado joined [I1], fit together [I29]

encajador person who inserts [II30]

encajar to join [I10], to fit [I22], to put [II17],to plunge [II20], to pass on [II43]

encaje: celada de — closed helmet [I1], **la ley de** — arbitrary law [I11]

encalabrinar to make one choke [II10]

encambronado serious and erect [II56]

encaminando directing [II64]

encaminar to guide [I2], to lead to [I16], to take [I27], to drive [I33], —se to go toward [I1]

encamisado wearer of surplice [I19]

encantado enchanted [I1]

encantador enchanter [prI]

encantamento = **encantamiento** enchantment [I1], **por** — as by magic [II19]

encantar to enchant [I6]

encanto enchantment [I22]

encarado aimed [II27]

encaramarse to climb up [II14]

encarecer to overrate [prI], to enhance [I11], to extol [I13], to describe [I17], to stress [I47

encarecidamente earnestly [II1]

encarecido flattering [I24]

encarecimiento exaggeration [I27], praises [aprob. II]; **con** — ardently [I9]

encargar to charge [I27], to burden [I4], to entrust [I40]

encarnado red [I27], flesh-colored [II49]

encarnizado flashing [II31]

encasquetarse to put a hat on [I27]

encastillado fortified [I34]

encender to inflame [I7], to light [I16]

encendido burning [I4]

encerado waxed [II18]

encerrado locked up [I24], in seclusion [I25], included [I33], enclosed [II53]

encerramiento locking-up [I12], cloistered life [I28]

encerrar to conceal [I34], to embrace [I11], to be enclosed [I42], to hold [I46], to include [II49], **—(se)** to shut (oneself) up [I3]

encierro seclusion [I28], hiding

place [II54]

encima de on [I8], above [II8]

encina evergreen oak tree [I4]

encinar oak grove [II10]

encinta pregnant [II52]

enclavar to pierce [I34]

enclavijar to lock [I38]

encoger to shrug [I18], to contract [I20], to rumple [I38], to hunch up [II26]

encogido cowering [I46], confined [II7], hunched over [II47]

encolerizado angry [I19]

encomendado commended [I5]

encomendar to commend [I7], to commit to another's protection [I25], to entrust [I14], to remember [someone to someone

encomendar, cont'd. else] [II50], **a —** with compliments [I22]

enconar to get through treachery [I27]

encontinente immediately [I42/43]

encontrarse to meet [I1], to clash [I18]

encorporado = incorporado obstinate [I48]

encorvamiento curving [II14]

encrucejadas = encrucijadas crossroads [I4]

encrucijadas crossroads [I21]

encuadernado bound [I6]

encubertado draped [II35]

encubierto hidden [I23], secret [II63]

encubrir to conceal [prI]

encuentro blow [I1], encounter [I33], unlucky throw in dice [I25]

encumbrado lofty [II30]

encumbrarse to be bombastic [II26]

endeble weak [I16]

endecha dirge [I12]

endechadera hired mourner [II7]

endechar to lament [II67]

endemoniado devilish [I38], possessed by the devil [II47]

enderezador righter [I52]

enderezar to rectify [I2], to straighten [I22], to set right [I29], to make for [I41], to direct [II42], **—se** to straighten up [I8]

endiablado perverse [I6], bedeviled [I8]

endriago dragon [I25]

endrigo = endriago dragon [II8]

endurecer to make hard [I28]

endurecido hardened [II35]

enemigo enemy [prI]

enemistad hatred [I7]

enfadar to vex [I22], to offend [I3], **—se** to become angry [prI]

enfado vexation [I5]

enfadoso vexatious [I12]

enfermedad illness [I5]

enfermo sick [I4]; sick person [I21]

enflaquecer to become weak [I1]

enfrascarse to engage [I1]

enfrenado bridled [I23]

enfrenar to bridle [I31]

enfriar to make cold [II17], —**se** to get cold [I11]

engañado deceived [I17], enticed [II13]

engañador deceiver [II33]

engañar to cheat [I3], to deceive [I21], —**se** to be deceived [I3]

engañifa deception [II2]

engaño misconception [prI], deceit [I11], deception [I6], **llamarse a** — to claim that one has been deceived [I46]

engañoso deceitful [II21]

engastado set (as jewels) [I41], sunken [II32]

engendrar to beget [prI], to engender [I34]

engolfado on the high seas [I41]

engolfar to be engaged in arduous affairs[II42]

engrandecer to extol [I27]

engullir to gorge [I24]

enhilar to thread [I25], to link together [I22]

enhorabuena congratulations [II56]

enhoramala bad luck [II31]

enjaezado decorated [II72]

enjalma light packsaddle [I16]

enjambre beehive [II5]

enjaulado caged [I47]

enjaular to put in a cage [I47]

enjuagarse to rinse [II59]

enjugar to dry [II19]

enjundia fat [II4]

enjuto dry [I34], **a pie** — in comfort [II5]

enlazado bound [I21]

enlazar to bind [I34]

enlutado mourner [I19]

enmantar to cover [II48]

enmendar to rectify [I24], correct type [II62]

enmudecer to become silent [I20], to make silent [I24]

enoblecer = ennoblecer to honor [I27]

enojado angry [I9]

enojar to bother [I41], —**se** to get angry [I11], to anger [II1], to become vexed [II41]

enojo anger [I2], vexation [I15], annoyance [I29]

enramada bower [II19]

enramar to screen with branches [II19]

enredado tangled [II58]

enredar to tangle [II58], —**se** to join [II20]

enredo deception [II10]

enrejado with grate [I42/43]

enriquecer to get rich [I8], to enrich [I48], to endow [I50]

enristrar to couch a lance [I19]

enrizado curly [I26]

enroscado coiled [II58]

ensabanado sheeted [I52]

ensalada salad [I16]

ensalmo incantation [I29]

ensalzamiento exaltation [I31]

ensalzar to exalt [I11]

ensanchar to enlarge [I52], to cheer [II10]

ensanche appendix [II8]

ensangrentado bloodied [II58]

ensarmentar to bury vines so they'll take root [II53]

ensartado strung together [I22]

ensartar to string together [I2]

ensayar to rehearse [I41]

enseñado taught [I2], instructed [I48]

enseñar to show [I26], to teach [II27]

ensillar to saddle [I1]

ensordecer to deafen [II74]

ensuciar to make dirty [I33]

entablado splinted [II53]

entabladura carved form wood [II58]

entablarle to splint [II14]

entallar to sculpt [II12], —se to be sculpted [I2]

ente being [II35]

entena lateen yard [II62]

entendedor understander [II37]

entender to tend to [I17], **dar a** — to make understand [I3], **darse a** — to convince oneself [II24]

entendido understood [I2], wise [prI], intelligent [I11]; connoisseur [aprob. II]

entendimiento intellect [prI], understanding [I6], judgment [I11], senses [II38]

entera virgin [II59]

enterado informed [I21], convinced [II19]

enterar to inform [I14], —se to verify [I33]

entereza virginity [I24], integrity [I34], wholeness [II11]

enternecer to move [I20], to make tender [II20], —se to be moved [I41]

entero whole [I1], preserved [II8]

enterrar to bury [I12], to be buried [I23]

entibiar to moderate passions [I34], to moderate [I37]

entierro burial [I12]

entomecer = **entumecer** to make numb [I19]

entonado in tune [I42], conceited [II5], haughty [II19]

entonarse to be conceited [II5]

entonces then [I1]

entono haughtiness [I9], conceit [I5]

entorpecer to stupefy [II49]

entrada entrance [I27]

entrambos both [I15]

entrañas bowels [I11], heart [I41]

entrar to enter [I2], to plunge [I34], to take in [I34], to bear down [I39], to escort [II31]; — **a la parte** to share [I40]

entre among [I3], during [II12], in [II23], — **sí** to himself [I5], **días de** — **semana** weekdays [I1]

entrecano greying [II14]

entreclaro fairly light [II9]

entredicho interdiction [I25]

entrega delivery [I23], surrender [II1]

entregado given up [I8]

entregar to hand [prI], to deliver [reI]

entrego = **entrega** [II1]

entremés one-act comic play [pról. II]

entremeter to insert [II68], **se** to occupy oneself [I25], to engage in [I30], to meddle [I31]

entremetido mixed [II18]

entreoír to overhear [I45]

entreparecer to glimpse [II36]

entresacar to make a clearing [II67]

entretanto while [I4], meanwhile [I6]

entretejerse to insert oneself [II30]

entretejido intertwined [I11]

entretener to entertain [I14], to delay [I24], to spend time [I28], to allay [I33], to sustain [I38];

—**se** to defend oneself [I44], to waste time [II3], to maintain [II24]

entretenido maintained [I8], occupied [I42], entertaining [II44], wards off hunger [II54], **mal** — loafing [II49]; prankster [II32]

entretenimiento recreation [I24], occupation [I40], pension [II24]

entreverado mixed [II18]

entricado = **intricado** obscure [I1]

entristecer to sadden [II5], —**se** to become sad [I22]

entronizado enthroned [II34]

enturbiar to muddy [I25]

envainar to sheathe sword [I45]

envaramiento constables with their staffs [II26]

envasar to drink [I17]

enviar to send [I1]

envidar to parley [I4]

envidia envy [I7]

envidiado envied [I14]

envidiar to envy [I8]

envidioso envious [I17]

envilecer to debase [I16]

envite invitation [II3]

enviudar to become a widower [II42]

envolver to cover [II20]

envuelto wrapped up [I19], mixed up [I35]

epigrama epigram [prI]

episodio episode [I28]

epitafio epitaph [I39], inscription [II45]

equidad fairness [II3]

equinocial, línea equator [II29]

equivalente similar [I25], equivalent [II7]

era threshing floor [I25]

erario treasury [aprob. II]

erguido staunch [II13]

erguir to stand up [II35]

erizado rigorous [I13]

erizarse to stand on end [I19]

ermita shrine [I52], hermitage [I52]

ermitaño hermit [II24]

errar to go astray [I48], to go [I522], —**se** to make a mistake [I20]

errata mistake [erratas I]

erudición learning [dedI]

erudito learned [prI]

erutación belch [II43]

erutar to belch [II43]

esaminadores = examinadores examiners [II1]

escabroso craggy [I23]

escala staircase [II53], ladder [II62]

escalera staircase [I21], stairs [I6]

escalón stair [I34], step [II16]

escamondar to trim trees [II67]

escamoso scaly [I14]

escanciador wine waiter [I49]

escanciar to pour wine [II23]

escandalizarse to scandalize [II62]

escaño bench [II33]

escaparse to escape [I42/43]

escaramuza skirmish [I16]

escarbar to scrape [II1]

escardar(se) to weed [I6]

escarlata scarlet [II31]; scarlet cloth [I21]

escarmenar to learn from experience [II74]

escarmenar to comb [I23]

escarmentado person who has learned from experience [I50]

escarmentar to learn a lesson [pról. II], to take warning [I23]

escarnecer to ridicule [I22]

escarnidos = escarnecidos deceived [II21]

escarolado frilled [II44]

escarpines socks [II35], slippers [II44]

escaseza = escasez stinginess [I47]

escaso scanty [I33]

esclavina short cape [II54]

esclavo slave [I22]

escocer to smart [II35]

escogido chosen [II50]

escogido chosen [I6], select few [I48]

escolar scholar [I12]

esconder to hide [I4]

escondido hidden [I16], deceptive [I18]

escondimiento hiding [I34]

escondrijo hiding place [II57]

escopeta musket [I18], — **de rueda** flintlock [I22]

escopetero rifleman [II63]

escoplo chisel [II45]

escote share [I26]

escrebir = **escribir** [I3]

escremento growth [II43], —**s mayores** bowel movements [II23]

escribano notary [I22], — **de cámara** clerk of a court of justice [tasa I]

escrito writing [I13]

escritorio drawer [I8], **por** — written out [II43]

escritura writing [prI], record [I25]

escrúpulo qualm [I13]

escrupuloso frightened [I21], hypercritical [I34], laden with qualms [II1], scrupulous [II26]

escrutinio scrutiny [I6]

escrutiñador *modern* **escudriñador** censor [I7]

escuadra military squad [I39]

escuadrón squadron [I18], — **volante** renegade troops [II11]

escudarse to protect oneself [I22]

escudería squiring [I52]

escuderil squirely [prI]

escudero squire [prI]

escudilla bowl [I6]

escudillar to serve oneself [II28]

escudo gold coin [I23], shield [I2]

escudriñador investigator [II22]

escudriñar to scrutinize [I23], to search [I52]

escuela school [II7]

escueto simple[II5]

esculpirse to be sculpted [I2]

escupir to spit [II13]

escuras, a in the dark [II13]

escurecer = **obscurecer** to confuse [prI], to dim [I20], to obscure [pról II], —**se** to grow dark [I12]

escuridad = **oscuridad** darkness [I19]

escurísimo very dark [II55]

escuro = **oscuro** dark [I14]

escurriendo = **discurriendo** going on [I26]

escurrir = **discurrir** to roam [II52]

escusa = **excusa** excuse [I6]

escusado = **excusado** useless [I14], superfluous [II70], **no** — crucial [II70], inevitable [II73], **pensar en lo** — to make a mistake [II4]

escusar = **excusar** to avoid [I5], to omit [I11], to fail [II52]

esencia, de necessary [I20]

esentar = **exentar** to exempt [prI]

esento = **exento** free [I40]

esferas heaven [II7]

esfogar = **desfogar** to reduce flames [I34]

esforzado valiant [I19]

esforzar to encourage [I24], to

exert [I41], —se to make an effort [I14]

esfuerzo courage [I2], strength [I3]

esgremir = esgrimir to brandish [I19]

esgrima, de for fencing [II19]

esgrimir to brandish [II11], to fence [I19]

eslabón link [I34]

eslabonar to link [II13]

esmeralda emerald [I50]

esorbitante exorbitant [II17]

esotro this other [I25], that other [I6]

espaciarse to relax [I42]

espacio period of time [I3], time [II1], distance [I8], ledge [II23], **con tanto** — as slowly [I37], **de** — slowly [II50]

espaciosísimo very wide [II61]

espacioso wide [I2], slow [II38]

espada sword [I1], swordsmanship [II19]

espalda shoulder [I15], shoulder blades [II1]; **-s** back [I22], shoulders [I16], back [I22], **volver las** — to turn around [I14], **a las** — on their backs [I8], **a sus** — behind him [I47]

espaldar backplate [I2], back of chair [II47]

espaldarazo slap on the back [I3]

espalder principal rower [II62]

espantable frightful [I8]

espantadizo skittish [II35]

espantado frightened [I27], amazed [II25], **de** — in amazement [I2]

espantajo frightening apparition [II36], deterrent [II51]

espantar to chase away [I22], to frighten [I45], —se to become frightened [I19], to be astonished [I32]

espanto fright [I20], astonishment [I40]

espantoso frightening [II17]

esparcido scattered [prI]

esparcir to scatter [I14]

esparraguera asparagus plant [I18]

esparto mat-weed [prI]

especia spice [II20]

especial especially [I4]

especie spice [II47]

especular to examine [II22]

espediente resolution [II64]

espejo mirror [prI]

esperado eagerly awaited [II56], **no** — unexpected [I22]

esperante person who waits [II17]

esperanza hope [I11]

esperar to hope [I2], to wait for [I33], to expect [I42/43], to trust [II19]

esperezare to stretch [II68]

esperiencia = experiencia experience [II1]

espeso thick [I23]

espesura dense part [I4]

espetáculo spectacle [II26]

espetado spitted [II20]

espetera rack [II74]

espía spy [I39]

espiga ear of wheat [I18]

espilorchería stinginess *Ital.* [II24]

espina thorn [I31]

espinazo backbone [I9]

espirado = expirado expired [II21]

espirar = expirar to expire [II21]

espíritu mind [I32], soul [prI], spirit [I17]

espléndido splendid [II21]

esplendor splendor [II24]

espolear to spur [I20]

espolón point of prow [I38]

esponja sponge [I39]

esposa wife [I5], —**s** handcuffs, manacles [I22]

esposo husband [I23]

espreso express [II25]

espuela spur [I3]

espulgar to examine [II60]

espuma skimmings [II20], cream [I22], foam [II34]

espumar to skim [II20]

esquero esquero [II27]

esquife skiff [I41]

esquila (cow) bell

esquilón cowbell [II22]

esquina street corner [I14]

esquisito rich (as food) [II49]

esquivarse, to disdain [I12], to avoid [I41]

esquiveza = esquivez aloofness [I33]

esquivo elusive [I14]

estable permanent [I27]

establecido established [II12]

establo stable [I16]

estaca stake [I11]

estacada dueling place [I33]

estacazo blow with a stake [I15]

estación devotional visit to church [I33]

estaciones, andar to come back [II1]

estada stay [I46]

estado profession [I1], rank [I15], estate [I24], position [I41], state [II6], condition [I13], status [II19], height of average man [II23]; **materias de —** affairs of state, **poner en —** to marry off a child [I51], **razón de —** politics [II1]

estambre de la vida course of life [II38]

estampa print shop [II22], printing presses [II62], **en —** in print [II3], **dar a la —** to publish [I3]

estampado imprinted [II48]

estampero engraver [II62]

estancia dwelling [I23], stanza [I33], room [I42]

estanco stop [II14]

estandarte flag [I39], banner [II27]

estante = **instante** [I26]

estanterol captain's station [I39], beam to which mast cords are attached [II63]

estaño tin [I38], lagoon [I38]

estar to lie [II62], — **por** to feel like [I33]

estatua statue [I33]

estatuido ordained [I33]

estatura height [II1]

estatuto statute [II53]

estender = **extender** to extend [I12]

estendido = **extendido** spacious [I18], exaggerated [II25]

estenso = **extenso: por** — in detail [I20]

estera de enea rush mat [I16]

estercolar to sped manure [II12]

estéril barren [prI]

esterilidad sterility [II22]

estevado bowlegged [II1]

estiércol manure [II12]

estigio lago River Styx [II69]

estil *corruption of* **estéril** barren [I12]

estilo style [prI]

estima esteem [I25]

estimación esteem [I24], appraisal [I33]

estimado esteemed [I6]

estimar to value [II11], to

appreciate [II16], to consider [II21]

estío summer [II53]

estirado stretched out [I42/43], elevated [I18]; haughty person [II27]

estirarse to stretch oneself [I42/43]

estirpe lineage [II20]

estocada straight thrust [II19]

estómago stomach [I8]

estopa bandage [I16], **copo de** — tuft of flax [II5]

estoque rapier [I15]

estorbar to prevent [I1]

estorbo impediment [I34]

estornudar to sneeze [I11]

estornudo sneeze [II44]

estotro = **este otro** [I18]

estrado drawing room [I33]

estrago havoc [I37]

estrambote refrain [II38]

estranjero = **extranjero** foreign [I21]; foreigner [II54]

estrañeza = **extrañeza** strange thing [I13], strangeness [I24]

estraño = **extraño** singular [I1], strange [I1]

estraordinariamente very much [I42/43]

estraordinario = **extraordinario** extraordinary [I28]

estrategema strategy [I37]

estrechamente tightly [I23]

estrechar to force [I48]

estrecheza (*mod.* **estrechez**) narrowness [I27], poverty [I39], rigidity [II18]

estrechísimamente very tightly [I21]

estrechísimo very austere [II18]

estrecho austere [I13], narrow [I16], straits [I41], strict [II57], miserly [I39], tight [II62]

estregar to scratch [II10]; **que te estrego, burra de mi suegro** (indicates impatience) [II10]

estrella star [I1]

estrellar(se) to smash [II44]

estremadamente very well [I48]

estremado consummately good [I10], extreme [I51], incomparable [II23]

estremarse = extremarse to exert oneself [I14]

estremecerse to stretch [II4]

estremo = extremo extreme [I24], of the highest degree [I13]; tip [I4/43]; **por/en todo —** extremely [I40], very well [II27]

estrépito noise [I20]

estribar to lie [I52]

estribo stirrup [I2], **perder los —** to talk nonsense [I49]

estricote, al from pillar to post [I26]

estripaterrones clodhopper [II50]

estropajo useless person [II68]

estropeado mutilated [I9]

estropear to mutilate [II26]

estruendo pomp [I1], clatter [I7], noise [I20]

estuche sheath [I29], needle case [II48]

estudiantado paje mischievous page [I2]

estudiante studious [II58]

estudio study [I48]

estupendo stupendous [II36]

etéreo ethereal [II8]

eternamente eternally [I16]

eternizar to immortalize [I47]

eterno eternal [I1]

ético consumptive [I9]

etiope Ethiopian [I18]

evangelio New Testament [prI], **cuatro —s** gospels [I10]

evidencia evidence [I48]

evitar to avoid [I7]

exageración exaggeration [II58]

exagerar to extol [I27], to exaggerate [I42/43]

examen examination [I48]

examinado licensed [II45]

exceder to exceed [I48]

excelencia excellence [II22], **vuestra —** you [dedI]

excetando = exceptuando excepting [II58]

exclamar to exclaim [II17]

exequia funeral rite [II19]

exequias funeral rites [II31]

exorbitancia exorbitance [II51]

experiencia experiment [I1], trial [I2], proof [I15], experience [I21]

experimentado experienced [II23]

experimentar to experience [II54]

expreso express [II12]

exprimir to squeeze [II17]

extirpar to wipe out [aprob. II]

extraño foreign [prI]

extraordinario extraordinary [II59]

extremo extreme [I24], of the highest degree [I13]; tip [I42/43]; **por/en todo —** extremely [I40]

F

fábrica manufacture [II62]

fabricado made I16 [II62]

fabricador creator [I35]

fabricar to devise [I40], to make [II6], to make up [I24]

fábula fable [prI], plot [I47]

fabuloso fictitious [prI], incredible [prI]

facción battle [II24], **—s** features [II32]

face = hace [I21]

facer *arch.* **hacer** [I2]

faceto amusing [aprob. II]

facienda = hacienda [I26]

facilidad ease [I1], with ease,
haste [I19], ready compliance [II21], **con —** easily [I19]

facilitar to supply [I10], to manage [I33], to alleviate [I40], to facilitate [I44]

facinoroso = facineroso wicked [I27]

facion = facción battle [I51], facial features [II1]

facultad right [reI]

fada = hada fairy [I50]

faisán pheasant [II49]

faja border [I27], diaper [II73]

fajar to bind [II22]

falda skirt [I10], tail of skirt [II5], side of mountain [I25], **—s** tail of shirt [I26], **perrilla de —** lapdog [II25]

faldamento skirt [II19]

faldellín skirt [II23]

faldriquera pocket [II14]

fallar = hallar [I5]

falsario liar [II3]

falsía fraud [II16]

falso false [I18], counterfeit [II3]

falta defect [prI], fault [I4], lack [I18], **— de** lacking in [prI]

faltar to lack [prI], to not fulfill [I14], to fail [I18], to be away [I34], to be missing [I35]; **— a la palabra** to break one's word [I16]

falto: de juicio crazy [I46], **— de memoria** lacking in memory [II8]

faltriquera puse [II73]

fama fame [I1], opinion [I14], **es — ** it is said [I6], **buena — ** reputation [I33]

familiar well-known [I35], personal devil [II5]

famoso notable [I13], remarkable [I13]

fanal lantern [I39]

fanega 1.6 bushels [II13]

fanfarrón show-off [I47]

fantasía imagination [I1], vanity [II50]

fantasioso stuck up [II50]

fantasma phantom [I17]

fantástico unreal [I17]

faquín laborer [I30]

farándula acting profession [II11]

fardo bale [II43]

farol lantern [II61]

farsante actor [II11]

farseto quilted jacket worn under armor [I21]

fasta *arch.* **hasta** until [I2]

fastidio boredom [II26]

fatal fatal [II21]

fatiga distress [I22]

fatigado bothered [I3],weary [I17]

fatigar to bother [I2], to distress [I34], to exert [I42/43]

favor protection [I4], support [I22], signs of affection [II19], **carta de — ** letter of recommendation [I47]

favorecer to favor [dedI], to protect [I7], to befriend [I11], to help [II21]

favorecido favored, above the law [II11]

favorido favorite [I37] *arch.*

faz face [I2]

fazaña *arch.* **hazaña** [I2]

fe certificate [erratas I], faith [approb. ii], affidavit [reI], testimony [dedI]; **dar — ** to attest [tasa I], **a — ** in truth [I6], **a — de** on one's honor, **a buena — ** honestly and sincerely [I21]

fealdad foul act [I34], ugliness [II10]

fecho *arch.* made [reI], done [I2]; feat [I20]

fechoría misdeed [I52]

fechuría = fechoría mischief [II21], *arch.* deed [II48]

fecistes = hicisteis [I19]

fecunda fruitful [prI]

**fee = fe; a — ** in truth [I5];

felice = feliz happy [I8]

felicemente happily [II16]

felicísimamente very happily [I48]

felicísimo most fortunate [I4]

feligrés parishioner [I12]

fementido truthless [I8], treacherous [I16], fake [I18]

fender *arch.* to split [I9], *mod.* **hender**

fendiente cutting [I9]
fenecer to conclude [I35]
fenestra *arch.* window [I21]
fénix exquisite [I13]
feo ugly [prI]
feria market [II68]
feriar to buy [I24]
ferida *arch.* wound [I5]
ferido *arch.* wounded [I5]
fermoso *arch.* **hermoso** [I2]
fermosura *arch.* **hermosura** beauty [I1]
fermosura *arch.* beauty [II30]
ferocidad ferocity [I46]
feroz ferocious [I50]
ferreruelo *arch.* **herreruelo** cape [II71]
ferro anchor [II29]
fértil fertile [II42]
fertilidad fertility [II22]
fertilizar to nourish (with water) [II58]
ferviente boiling [I50]
festejar to regale [I33]
festivo witty [prI]
fiado trusting [I34]
fiador guarantor [I17]
fiambre coldcuts [I16]
fiambrera lunch basket [I19]
fianza bond [II68]
fiar to confide [I33], to vouch for [II1], to trust [II20], —**se** to trust [dedI]
ficieron = hicieron [I19]
fidedigno trustworthy [I52]

fidelidad loyalty [I33]
fidelísimo most loyal [II38]
fiel faithful [I19]; pointer on scale [II17]
fieltro, de calloused [II25]
fiera wild beast [I13]
fiereza fierceness [II58]
fiero fierce [I1]
fierro weapon [II32]
fiesta holiday [I1], festival [I19], enjoyment [I51]; **hacer** — to please [I42/43]
figura shape [I2], face [I4], figure [II19], —**se** to seem [I23], — **del artificio** puppet [II25]
figurarse to imagine [I19]
figurero astrologer [II25]
figurilla little figure [II26]
fijarse to make [II21]
fil point on scale where both sides are equal [II51]
filisteo Philistine [prI]
filo edge [I13]
filósofo philosopher [prI]
fin end [I22], object [I29], goal [I6], **al** — **de** at the end of [reI], **en** — finally [I24]
finalmente finally [II32]
fineza beauty, fineness, nice thing [I25]
fingidamente in a pretending way [I33]
fingido pretended [II23], pretend [II74]
fingimiento deceit [II21]

fingir to pretend [I24], to fancy [I27], to conceal intentions [I40]

finísimo very fine [I1]

fino fine [I1]

finojo = hinojo knee[I31]

finta, hacer to threaten [II39]

firma signature [I25], testimonial [I40]

firmado resolved [II63]

firmar to sign [II25]

firme firm [I16]

firmemente firmly [II8]

firmeza constancy [I24], stability [II62]

fiscal prosecutor [II19]

fisga banter [I20]

físico doctor [II71]

fisonomía physiognomy = face [II14]

fizo = hizo [I10]

flaco thin [I1], feeble [I13]

flamante brand-new [I2], magnificent [II44]

flamenco Flemish [II41]

flámula pennant [II61]

Flandes Flanders, modern Belgium [aprob. II]

flaqueza frailty [I20], weakness [I34], leanness [II16]

flauta flute [II19]

flecha arrow [I14]

flechar to aim a bow [II20]

flema apathy [I35], sluggishness [I47], calm [II17]

flemático sluggish [I23]

flexible flexible [II71]

flojamente laxly [II36]

flojedad sloth [II6]

flojo with loose clothing [II43], slouching [II43]

flor flower [I6]

floreciente blooming [I51]

florecilla little flower [II35]

floresta flowered forest [I8]

florido flowery [I50], blossoming [I35]

fócil (nonsense word) [II7]

folgar to fornicate [I19]

follón rogue [I3]

folloncico rogue [II74]

fondo bottom [II29], **dar —** to anchor [I41], to hit bottom [II55], **ir a —** to sink [I41]

fontecilla small spring [I31]

forajidos outlaw [II60]

forastero outsider [I51], stranger [II9]

forcejar to struggle [I16]

foribundo = furibundo raging [I18]

forjar to forge [I21]

forma position [II14]

formar to devise [I1], to make up [I20], to weigh heavily on one's conscience [I49], to form [II47]

fortalecer to strengthen [I28]

fortaleza strength [I1], fortress [I2], security [I41]

fortificación fortification [I40]

fortificar to strengthen [I1], to fortify [I45]

fortísimamente very strongly [II22]

fortísimo very strong [II36]

fortuna fortune [I6]

forzada raped one [II45]

forzado by force [I8], compelled [I17], sentenced [I22], raped [II48]

forzar to force [I11], to rape [II45]

forzosamente necessarily [I19]

forzoso necessary [I10], obligatory [I14]

forzudo strong [I25]

fosco gloomy [I30]

fracasar to destroy [I25]

fragancia fragrance [I31]

fragante, en in the act [I22]

fragata frigate [I41]

fragrancia = fragancia [I33]

fragua forge [II1]

fraguar to forge [II43]

fraile friar [I8]

frailecito little friar [II8]

francés Frenchman [II23]

franchote foreigner [II54]

franco exempt [I23], **campo —** open field [II56]

franja fringe [II44]

frasis language [I45]

fraude fraud [I11], deceit [I23]

frazada cover [I16]

frecuencia frequency [I33]

fregar to wash dishes [II32]

fregón,-ona dishwasher [I48]

freír to fry [I37]

frenético frenzied [I52]

frenillado with oars tied down, out of the water [I41]

freno bridle [I19], bit of horse [I33], restraint [II27]

frente forehead [prI]

fresco cool [I2], new [II7], fresh [II13]

frescor coolness [II20]

frescura coolness [I49]

fresno ash tree [I28]

fresquísima very cool [II23]

frialdad cold [II62]

frión dull [II72]

frisado napped [II38]

frisar to approach [I1], to diminish [I33], **por —** unnapped [II38]

friscal [a nonsense word] [II19]

frito fried [II20]

frondoso leafy [I50]

frontera front [II20]

frontero in front [I18]

fruncido wrinkled [II48]

fruta fruit [I41]], **— seca** dried fruit [I10]

fruto fruit [I1], effect [II17]

fuego fire [I6], **poner —** to set fire [II8]

fuelle bellow [II41]

fuente fountain [prI], spring [I12], basin [II32], issue [II48]

fuera outside [I2], — **de** outside of [II49], — **de sí** beside oneself [I44], **de** — untucked [II24]

fuera = sería [I34]

fuero law [I17]

fuerte strong [I1], fort [I39]

fuertemente strongly [I42/43]

fuerza need [I2], virtue, violence [I15], strength [I32], power [I38], fortress [I38], fort [I39]; **por** — by force [I7], force [I22], **hacerse** — to struggle with self [I34], **es** — it is necessary [II20]

fuesa grave [II74]

fuga torrent [I27], flight [I49]

fugitivo fleeing [I46], perishable [II41]

fullero cheater [II49]

funda sheath [I49]

fundado founded [prI], based [I33]

fundador founder [II8]

fundamento foundation [I16]

fundar to set up [II13], —**se** to be based on [II8]

fundar to base an opinion [I33], to found [I48]

fundir to melt [I21]

funesto mournful [I14], funereal [II21]

furia rage [I4], fury [I8]

furibundo raging [I46]

furioso raving [I25], fierce [II47]

furto, a on the sly [I16]

futuro future [I2]

fuyades =*arch. for* **huyáis** flee [I8]

fuyáis *arch.* **huyáis** flee [I4]

fuyan *arch.* **huyan** flee [I2]

G

gabán sleeved cloak [I17], overcoat [I22]

gacha mush [II17]

gafo leprous person [II29]

gaita zamorana hurdy-gurdy [II20]

gala festive [I27], elegance [II1], full dress [I11], military dress uniform [I51]; —**s** uniforms and accessories [I39]

galán,-ana handsome [II1]; handsome young man [woman] [I51]

galano splendidly dressed [I33]; elegant [I50]

galápago tortoise [II53]

galeota small galley [I41]

galeote galley slave [I22]

galera galley [I6]

galería gallery [I42/43]

galgo greyhound [I1]

galiciano Galician [I15]

gallardar to sit up straight [II30]

gallardete pennant [II61]

gallardía gracefulness [I16], gallantry [II11]

gallardo gallant [prI], lively [I9],

charming [I42]

gallego Galician (from northwestern Spain) [I15]

gallina chicken [I19]

gallipavo imported turkey [I11]

gallo rooster [I11]

galocha cap with flaps [II48]

galope gallop [I8], trot [I52], **de — ** hurriedly [I3]

gamella arched extremity of yoke [I11]

gamo deer [I21]

gana desire [I4], **de buena —** with pleasure [I4], **de mala —** reluctantly

ganadero cattle owner [I20]

ganado cattle [I12], mounts [I14], **— mayor**, oxen, cows, **— de cerda** pigs [II45]

ganancia profit [I12], acquisition [I21]; **no le arrendara la —** I wouldn't like to be in their shoes [II1]

ganancioso winner [II49]

ganapán handyman [I48], porter [II13]

ganar to win [I7], to earn [I21]

gancho snag [II34]

gangoso speaking with a twang [I20]

ganso goose [II20]

gañán rustic [I30]

gañir to scream [II48]

garbanzo chickpea [I12]

garbear to pillage [I38]

garganta throat [I22], **— del pie** ankle [I41]

garito gambling house [II49]

garnacha juridical robe [II16]

garra claw [I46]

garrancho thorn

garrido elegant [II21]

garrotazo blow with club [I52]

garrote club [II14]

garza heron [II41]

gasaje = agasajo graceful reception [I11]

gasajo graceful reception [II32]

gascón from Gascony (SW France) [II54]

gascona, capa hooded cape [II26]

gastado wasted [I33]

gastador spender [I39], spoiler [II6]

gastar to spend [I23], to waste [I25], to spoil [I25], to wear [II35], to wear away [I51], to use [II14], to wear out [II40]

gasto expense [I17]

gata she-cat [II7]

gatas, a on all fours [I52]

gateamiento "catting" [II51]

gatear to scratch [II69]

gatesco catt-ish [II48]

gato cat [I8]

gatuno feline [II46]

gayadas motley [II44]

gaznatico windpipe *dim.* [I30]

gemidico little sigh [II49]

gemido sigh [I27]

gemir to moan [I27]
generación race [I1]
general general [II62]
género kind [I3], genre [I22], race [I40], type [prI], — **humano** human kind [I3]
generoso noble [I13], generous [I50], full-bodied [wine] [II20]
gente people [I4], gentile [II58]
gentil genteel [I2], graceful [I4], excellent [I22], pagan [I33]
gentiles, de of paganism [I12]
gentileza refinement [I13], elegance [I16]
gentilhombre gentleman [II1]
gentilidad paganism [I13], pagans [II8]
geometría geometry [II1]
gerifalte, como un perfectly [II34]
gigantazo great giant [I21]
gigante giant [prI]
giganteo gigantic [I1]
gigantillo giant [I37]
gilecuelco captive's jacket [I41]
gimio = simio monkey [I11]
ginovés Genoese [I39]
girifalte = gerifalte gerfalcon [II41], **como un** — very well [II32]
gitano gypsy [II4]
globo globe [II29]
gloria glory [I8]
glosa poetic gloss [II16]
glosar to gloss [II18]

glotón glutton [II20]
gobernador governor [I7]
gobernadora governor's wife [II5]
gobernadoresco pertaining to a governor [II55]
gobernar to manage [I33], to govern [II3], to control [II40]
gobiernito little government [II50]
gobierno management [I2], **buen** — common sense
godo Gothic [I18]
gola gorget [I28], throat [II39]
golfo high seas [I22], sea [I30]
golondrina swallow [I13]
golosazo glutton [II2]
golosina covetousness [I23], gluttony [II17]
goloso sweet-toothed [II4], glutton [II62]
golpe blow [I1], **de (un)** — all at once [I29], — **de agua** concussion of water [I20], **cerrar de** — to slam shut [I44]
golpear hammering [I20]
gomia waster [I39]
gordo fat [I2], large [II50]
gordura fatness [II43]
gorjear to chirp [II14]
gorra cap [I20]
gota drop [I3]
gótico Gothic [I52]
gozar (de, a) to enjoy [I12], to come to possess [I21]

gozo joy [I4]

gozoso delighted [I37]

grabado engraved [I12]

grabar to engrave [I26]

gracia cuteness [prI], grace [prI], cleverness [I30], gift [I39], favor [I39], skill [II19], name [II31]; **hacer —** to exempt [I4], **de —** gratis [I14], **de buena —** of good looks; **—s** thanks [I4]

graciosico funny [II49]

graciosísimo very pleasing [I7]

gracioso witty [prI], funny [I2], graceful [I2], amusing [II25]

grada step [II69]

grado station [I15], step [I21], stage of proceedings [I16], pleasure [I25], extent [I33], degree [I37], **mal de su —** against one's wishes [I8], **de —** willingly [I22]

graduado graduated [I1]

graduar to graduate [II22]

grajo crow [I23]

gramático grammarian [prI]

grana linen [II19]

grande grandee [I21]

grandeza greatness [dedI], great thing [I25], size [II1], **vuestra — your greatness = you [I1]; —s** great deeds [I12]

grandílocuo grandiloquent [II3]

grandiosidad grandeur [II8]

grandioso grandiose [I49]

grandísimo very great [I2], very big [I8]

grandor size [II66]

grangería gains [II54]

granizo hail [II19]

granjear to favor [dedI], to earn [I21], to win [II3], to gain [II24]

granjería gain [I12]

grano grain [I4], tuft [II38], seed [II41]

grasiento filthy [I35]

gratificado rewarded [I20]

gratificar to reward [I47]

grato free [I17]

grave important [prI], grave [I13]; serious person [prI]

gravedad composure [I9], seriousness [I33]

gravísimo very serious [I22]

graznar cawing [I14]

greba shin armor [I22]

gregüescos breeches [II24]

gremio fraternity [I40], bosom [I49], guild [II38]

griego Greek [I16]

grifo griffin [II58]

grillo cricket [II73], **—s** shackles [II49]

grita shouting [II6]

gritar to shout [I17]

grito shout [I21], **a —s** by shouting [I23]

grosero rustic [I11], **a lo —** in general terms [II71]

grueso large [I14]

grumete cabin boy [I40]

gruñidora grunting [II74]
gruñir to grunt [II9], to growl [II13]; grunting [II68]
gruta cave [II55]
guadamecil embossed leather [II71]
guadaña scythe [II19]
guante glove [I25]
guantero glovemaker [I31]
guarda guard, custody [I22], guardian [II23], —**-amigo** iron collar [I22], ¡—! be careful! [pról. II]
guardado reserved [I20], protected [I25]
guardar to keep [reI], to watch over [I4], to take care of oneself [I23]
guardarropas wardrobe [II34]
guardia, en keeping guard [I41]
guardián guard [I22]
guarismo Arabic number [I38]
guarnecido decorated [I23]
guarnición trimming [II21], **de** —**es** with set stones [II36]
¡guay! alas [II40]
guedeja lock of hair [I25]
guelte money *German* [II54]
güero vacant [I25]
guerra war [I8], **buena** — just war [I8]
guerrero warrior [I37]
güeso = hueso bone [II55]
güesped guest [I42]
güespeda innkeeper's wife [I41]

güevo egg *rustic* [II27]
guía guide [I41]
guiar to guide [I4], to conduct [I22]
guija pebble [II35]
guijarro pebble [I16], stone [I22]
guijeña stone [II35]
guilla good harvest [I12]
guirnalda garland [I13]
guisa manner [I22], degree [I25]
guisado prepared [I50]; arrangements [I51]
guisar to cook [II30]
guitarra guitar [I51]
guitarrista guitarist [II67]
gula gluttony [II8]
gulluría = gollería superfluity [I48]
gurapa galley [I22]
gusanillo little worm [I18]
gusano worm [II67]
gustar to taste [I3], to like [II2], — **de** to like [I23]
gusto pleasure [I1], taste [II3]
gustoso pleasing [I21]

H

ha = tiene has [I4]
haba bean [I32]
habedes *arch. for* **habéis** [I16]
habemos = hemos [I52]
haber to have [I18], to quarrel [II31], to act [II44]
haberes assets [I3]

habíades *arch. for* **habías**

hábil capable [I12], intelligent [I22]

habilidad talent [prI], cleverness [I6], ability [I50]

habitación dwelling [prI]

habitador dweller [prI]

habitar to dwell [I25]

habititar to enable [II52]

hábito dress [I12], order [I25], outfit [I44]

habla speech [II16]

hablado spoken [II20], **bien —** eloquent [I27]

hablador chatterbox [II3], talking [II62]

haca = **jaca** small horse [I15]

hacanea small horse [II30]

hacedero feasible [II21]

hacendoso industrious [I12]

hacer to play the part of [I29], to arrange [II55], **— cuenta** to calculate [I4], to figure [I6], to consider [I15], **— cuenta de** to pay attention [I25] **— fuera ropa** to have one take off one's shirt [II63], **— tienda** to raise a sail [II63], **— vela** to put up sails [II63]; **—se** to become [I1]

hacha torch [I18], hatchet [I9]

hacia towards [I4]

hacienda estate [I1], income [I1], wealth [I12], farm [I18], affairs [I26], work [II31]

hado fate [I14]

halagar to treat tenderly [II35]

halcón falcon [II10]

halda skirt [II50], **de -s o de mangas** one way or another [II51]

hallado found [I2]

hallador finder [II25]

hallar to find [I15], **—se** to be [prI], to be present [I42]

hallazgo treasure [I9], finding [I23], reward [I28]

hámago = **ámago** sour taste [ded. II]

hambre hunger [I2]

hambriento hungry [I13]

hanega = **fanega** 1.6 acres [I1], 1.6 bushels [I9]

harmonía harmony [I16]

harón sluggishness [II35]

harpa harp [I28]

harpado = **arpado** forked [I2]

harpar to tear [I21]

harpillera burlap [I16], saddle cloth [II22]

harrear to drive a mule [I17]

harriero muleteer [I2]

hartar to fill [I11], to satisfy [I42], **—se** to be satisfied [II20]

hartazga satiety [II47]

harto enough [I12], plenty of [I17], much [I23], quite [I52], full [II31], **—s** so many [I7]

hartura satiety [I37]

hasta up to [I4], even [I13], **— que** until. *See also* **fasta**

hato flock [I4], herd [II42]
haya beech tree [I12]
haz face [I20], bundle [I52]
hazaña deed [prI]
he = tengo [I18]
he aquí so [I31], here is, are [II25]
hebra lock of hair [I2], thread [I16]
hechicera witch [prI]
hechiceresco bewitched [II46]
hechicero sorcerer [I22]
hechizo enchantment [I22]
hecho deed [I2], feat [I20]; rendered [II11]; accustomed [I41], — **y derecho** full-fledged [I18]
hechura payment for tailoring [I45], workmanship [I50], shape [II8], part [II17], figure [II26]
heciste = hiciste [I23]
hediondo foul-smelling [II47]
helado frigid [I14]
helar to freeze [I22], —**se** to coagulate [I10]
hembra female [I41]
hender to split [I25]
heno hay [II3]
herbolario herbalist [II18]
herboso grassy [I52]
heredado inherited [I12]
heredero heir [I20]
hereje heretic [I5]
herida wound [I1]

herido wounded [I3], struck [I22]; wounded person [I3], **a campana herida** souding the alarm [I22], in public [II6]
herir to shine upon [I7], to hurt [I10], to wound [I34], to tremble [II14], to pierce [II58]
hermandad brotherhood [I23]
hermano brother [pról. I]
hermosear to make beautiful [I14]
hermosísimo very beautiful [I51]
hermoso beautiful [Iprol]
hermosura beauty [I25]
heroico heroic [I6]
herrado with spurs [I18]
herradura horse-shoe [I15], iron-clad [I18]
herrar to shoe a horse, **ténganos el pie al** — he should put us to the proof [II4]
herrería blacksmith's shop [I21]
herrero blacksmith [I21]
herreruelo cloak [I27]
hervir to boil [I11]
hidalga highborn lady [II5]
hidalgo member of lesser nobility, gentleman [I1]
hidalguía nobility [I34]
hideperro son of a dog [II3]
hideputa son-of-a-bitch [I25], bitch [I52]
hidiondo = hediondo foul-smelling [I47]
hidrópico hydropic [II20]

hiedra ivy [II20]

hielo ice [I13]

hierba grass [II12]

hierro iron [I1], head of lance [I8], knife [aprob. II], point [II26], —s iron implements [I10], —s iron bar [I22]

higa: no dar dis —s not to care a rap [I32]

hígado liver [II19]

higo fig [II8], **no se me da un — I** could care less [I8]

hijada flank [I18]

hijadear = ijadear = jadear to pant [I15]

hijito small child [II13]

hijo son [I6], —s children [I4]

hijodalgo = hidalgo [I12]

hila bandage [I3]

hilar to spin [I45]

hilacha thread [II58]

hilaza thread [II5], threadbare nature [II44]

hilera row [II20]

hilo thread [I4]

hincado stuck in the ground [II41]

hincapié, hacer to insist [II73]

hincar to drive [II14], —se de **rodillas** to kneel [I2]

hinchado inflated [II11]

hinchar to swell [prI]

hinchazón swelling [II38]

hinojo knee [I44]

hipérbole exaggeration [II17], exaggerated [II73]

hipocresía hypocrisy [II16]

hipócrita hypocritical [I11]

hipogrifo hippogriff [I46]

hirviendo boiling (*from* **hervir**) [I11]

hisopo sprinkler [I6]

historia story [prI], history [I48]

historiador historian [I6]

hito: tener la suya sobre el — to insist one is right [II10] (*see also* **mirar**), **dar en el —** to hit the nail on the head [II51]

hocicar to kiss [I46]

hocico snout [II13]

hogaño this year [II52]

hogaza loaf of bread [I18]

hoguera bonfire [I6]

hoja leaf [I1], sheet of paper [I48], **— de lata** tin [I12]

hojear to glance [I23], to turn the pages [II16]

hojuela cake [II69]

holanda fine linen [I15]

holgadamente comfortably [I46]

holgado at one's ease [I40]

holgar(se) to take pleasure [I1], to be glad [II5], to be pleased [I8], to have a good time [II62]

holgazán lazy person [II34]

hollar to tread on [II68]

hombre man [I2], **— de bien** good man [I7]

hombrecillo young man [II42]

hombrecito little man [II32]

hombro shoulder [I8]
hombrón big man [II34]
hombruno mannish [I31], man-like [I20]
homicida murderous [I13]
honda slingshot [I18]
hondo deep [I2]; **lo —** the depths
hondonada ravine [I23]
hondura depth [II55]
honestamente modestly [I11]
honestidad decency [I11], chastity [I11], modesty [I16]
honesto pure [prI], chaste [I4], modest [I25], reasonable [II16], honest [II16], in good taste [I43]
honra honor [dedI], glory [I3], chastity [I12]
honradísimo very honorable [II4]
honrado upright [prI], honorable [I5], reputable [I17]
honrar to honor [I24], **—se** to adorn oneself [I1], to wear [II24]
honroso honorable [I3]
hora time [I5], **a la buena —** happily [I3]
horadado pierced [I18]
horadar to bore [I2]
horca gallows [II51]
horcajadas, a astride [I32]
horcajadura crotch [I30]
horizonte horizon [I2]
horma shoemaker's last [I15]

hormiga ant [II12]
hornato = **ornato** embellishment [prI]
horno furnace [II6]
horrendo horrendous [I52]
horrísono terrifying noise [I20]; terrifying [II34]
horro clear [II52]
horror dread [I20]
hostalero innkeeper [I17]
hoto: vivir en — de otro to live under someone else's protection [II4]
hoy today [I7]
hoyo hole [II13], grave [II33]
hoz scythe [II53], **de — y de coz** suddenly [I45]
hubiere may have [reI]
hueco cave [I14], hollow area [I23], empty [II21], hollow [II34], vain [I62], **lo —** hollowed place [I11]
huele it smells, *from* **oler** [I13]
huella footprint [II21]
huérfano orphan [I11]
hueso bone [I15]
huésped innkeeper [I2], guest [I2], host [I3]
huéspeda innkeeper's wife [I32]
huevo egg [II7]
huid the one who fled [II17]
huida flight [I2]
huir(se) to flee [II12], to escape [I40]
humanista humanist [II22]

humano humane [prI], human [I8], secular [I48]

humedad dampness [II53]

humedecer to dampen [I19], to give moisture [I24]

húmedo radical semen [II47]

húmido = húmedo moist [I26]

humildad modesty [I3], meekness [I2], lowness [I28]

humilde humble [dedI], meek [I1]

humildemente humbly [II32]

humilisímo very humble [II38]

humillación bow [II69]

humillarse to humble oneself [I11], —**se** to bow [II42], **- la cerviz** to bow one's head

humo smoke [I6], —**s** taste [II37], **dar — a** to shine (shoes, with soot) [II2]

humor fluid [I25], disposition [I30], humor [I48]

hundido sunken [II7]

hundir to deafen [II56], —**se** to collapse [I15], to sink [I41]

huraño shy [II25]

hurón ferret [II16]

hurta: a — cordel on the sly [II32]

hurtado kidnaped [I8]

hurtar to steal [II4]

hurto robbery [I23]; **a —** by stealth [I24], on the sly [II62]; **a — de** undetected by [I42/43]

huso spinning-wheel spindle [I4]

I

ida visit [I33]

idea mind [II32]

ides = vais you are going [II26]**por**

idioma language [I6]

idiota foolish [I22]

ídolo idol [I1]

idóneo suited [II3]

iglesia church; — **mayor** cathedral [I9]

ignorado unknown [I5]

ignorancia ignorance [I6]

ignorante stupid [I33], ignorant [pról. II]

ignorar not to know [I8]

igual equal [I51], **sin —** matchless [I33]

igualar to equal [prI], to make equal [I11], —**se** to be equal [I18]

igualmente equally [II51]

ijada flank [II14]

ilustrado illustrated [I18]

ilustre noble [I27]

imagen image [I8]

imagin Zodiac sign [II29], image [II46]

imaginación thought [I8], mind [II34]

imaginado imagined [I22]

imaginar(se) to imagine [prI]

imaginativo pensive [prI]

imitación de, a in imitation of

[I2]
imitador imitator [I52]
imitar to imitate [I2]
impedimento impediment [I28]
impedir to prevent [I36], to stop [II17]
impeler to incite [I36], to propel [II63]
impenetrable impenetrable [II32]
impensado unexpected [I36]
imperatorio imperial [II42]
imperfeto incomplete [I27]
imperio right [I28], empire [I1], authority [I31]
imperioso powerful [II35]
impertinencia blunder [I6], impertinent remark [I51]
impertinente ill-advised[I33], irrelevant [II1]
ímpetu impulse [I8], fit [I20]
impío impious [II57]
impíreo = empíreo divine [I27]
implacable relentless [II1]
imponer to require [I31], —se to train [II55]
importar to be important [I1]
importunación insistent request [I36]
importunar to pester [I14], to beg earnestly [I51]
importunidad demand [I33], pleading [II42]
imposibilitado without means [I27], helpless [I31]

imposibilitar to render impossible [I15]
imposible impossible feat [II22]
imprenta print shop [pról. II]
impresión press-run [reI], printing [II22]
impreso printed [reI], been printed [II3]
impresor printer [reI]
imprimir to print [reI]
impropiedad inaccuracy [II26]
impropio incorrect [II26]
improvisamente suddenly [I14]
improviso, de/al suddenly [prI], im-provising [I18], "as he read" [I9]
imprudentemente carelessly [aprob. II]
impuesto imposed [I23]
impulso inspiration [II16]
inacabable endless [I1]
inacesible inaccessible [II18]
inadvertidamente inadvertently [I34]
inadvertido careless [II22]
inaudito unheard of [I37]
incansable tireless [I46]
incapaz incapable [prI]
incentivo incitement [I20]
incesable incessant [I20]
incierto uncertain [I14]
incitado spurred [I15]
incitar to stimulate [I25], to incite [I52]
incitativo incitement [II48],

stimulating thirst [II54]

inclemencia rigor [I11], **a las —s** in the open air [I15]

inclinación propensity [I51], bow of the head [II32]

inclinado disposed [I3], leaning [I20], bowed [II63]

inclinar to persuade [I28], to move [II35], to bow [II69], **—se** to bow [I40]

ínclito illustrious [I46]

incomodidad annoyance [prI], lack of comfort [I42]

incómodo discomfort [I17]

incomparable matchless [I27]

incomportable unbearable [II44]

inconsiderado inconsiderate [II21]

inconstancia inconstancy [I51]

incontrastable invincible [II1]

inconveniente obstacle [I10], trouble [pról. II], drawback [II44]

incredulidad incredulity [II14]

increíble incredible [I21]

incurrir to incur [reI], to fall [II13]

indecencia impropriety [II3]

indecente improper [I27]

indecible inexpressible [II42]

indicio indication [I11]

indigestión indigestion [I38]

indignación anger [I14]

indignado angry [I14]

indigno unworthy [I13]

indiscreto foolish [I13]

indomable unconquerable [II40]

indómito untamed [II35]

indubitable certain [I36]

indubitadamente undoubtedly [II1]

industria ingenuity [I1], stratagem [I32], cunningly [I40]; **de —** intentionally [I6]

industriado instructed [II31]

industriar to instruct [II54]

inefable incredible [II27]

inescrutable inscrutable [II32]

inestimable priceless [II16]

inexcusable indispensable [I33], inexcusable [I48]

inexpugnable impregnable [I46]

infacundo incoherent [I46]

infalible infallible [I34]

infamatorio discrediting [II1]

infame despicable [I4], infamous [II8]

infamia dishonor [I34]

infanta princess [I21]

infante boy [I4], prince [I7]

infantería infantry [I39]

inferir to infer [I13], to deduce [II6]

infierno hell [I14]

ínfimo lowest [I23]

infinidad boundlessness [I33]

infinito infinite [I14]; infinitely [II30]; **proceder en —** unending [II69]

influencia influence [II6]

influjo influence [I42/43]
informaciones testimony [II42]
informado informed [I29]
informar to inform [I27], —**se** to inform oneself [I5]
infortunio misfortune [II1]
infundir to instill [I3]
ingeniero engineer [I39]
ingenio state of mind [I33], talent [prI], wit [prI], cleverness [I22]; clever person [I8]
ingenioso visionary [tasa I]
ingerir to introduce [II44]
ingratitud unthankfulness [I13]
ingrato ungrateful [I14]
inhabilitado incapacitated [I50]
inhabitable uninhabitable [I23]
inhumanidad cruelty [I39]
injuria offense [I15], insult [II8]
injusto unjust [I18]
inmenso immense [II22]
inmortalidad immortality [II6]
inmundicia filth [I32]
inmundo filthy [II59]
innumerable countless [II1]; *see also* **inumerable**
inocente guiltless person [I6]
inominia = ignominia low state [II5]
inorme = enorme enormous [II36]
inquerir to investigate [I23]
inquieta to disturb [II19]
inquieto anxious [I42/43]

inquietud unrest [I13], calm [I36]
inquirir = inquerir to investigate [II52]
inremediable unsolvable [I34]
inreparable irrepairable [II32]
inresoluto = irresoluto indecisive [II21]
inseparable unbreakable [II19]
insidia snare [II34]
insigne distinguished [II3]
insignia designation [I19], device [I21], insignia [I47]
insolencia effrontery [I3], outrage [I25]
insolente insolent [I31], contemptuous [I41]
instabilidad = inestablidad instability [II53]
instable unstable [I14]
instante instant [I23], **al —** immediately [I2]
instigado incited [I17]
instituido instituted [I13]
instituir to establish [I11]
instrumento implement [I15]
insuficiencia inadequateness [prI]
insufrible unbearable [I13]
ínsula *arch.* island [I1]
insulano of an island [II13]
integridad integrity [II63]
intelegible intelligible [I33]
intención purpose [I22], view [I28], scheme [I34], opinion [I33], meaning [I41], intention

[I50], **buena** — good will [I46]

intencionado disposed [I4]; **bien** — good-natured [II13]

intenso intense [I35]

intentar to attempt [I33]

intento intention [I4], kindness [I24], **buen** — kindness [I24]

intercesor intercessor [II38]

interés interest [I9], concern [I11], what is due [I37], sum [I41], profit [II4], waelth [II20]

interesado interested [II71]

interesal interested [II49]

interese = interés [I11]

ínterin interim [I41]

intérprete interpreter [I9], translator [II44]

interromper = interrumpir to interrupt [I24]

interroto broken [II49]

interrumpir to interrupt [II3]

intervalo interval [II1]

intervención assistance [II36]

intervenir to get involved [II37]

intimación notification [II17]

intimar to summon [II7], to notify [II14]

íntimo depths [I36]

intitulado entitled [tasa I]

intonso novice [II70]

intrépido dauntless [I20]

intricable inextricable [I21]

intricadamente knottily [I22]

intricado intricate [I29], knotty [II45]

intricar to tangle [prI]

introducir to introduce [II43]

inumerabilidad = innumerabilidad innumerableness [prI]

inumerable innumerable [I17]

inusitado unaccustomed [I34]

inútil useless [I11]

invectiva censure [prI]

invencible invincible [I21]

invención fiction [I1], artifice [prI], contrivance [I11], pantomime [II21], deception [I37]

invenerable erroneous word for **invencible** [I37]

inventor inventor [I46]

invictísimo very invincible [I39]

invidia = envidia envy [aprob. II]

invidiado envied [II27]

invidiar = envidiar to envy [II16]

invidioso = envidioso envious [pról. II]

invierno winter [I38]

invito unconquered [I52]

invocar to invoke [II58]

ir: hacer — to chase away [I41], — **y venir en** to think about [II29]

ira rage [I40], wrath [II67]

irritar to irritate [II17]

islilla collar bone [I34]

izar to hoist [II63]

izquierdear to rave [II26]

J

jabalí wild boar [II34]

jabón soap [II32]

jabonadura lather [II32]

jabonar to satirize [II1]

jacinto jacinth [orange gem] [I50]

jadear to pant [I52]

jaez kind [I17], horse trappings [I44]

jalde bright yellow [I18]

jamás ever [I3]

jáquima headstall [I46]

jara dart [II23]

jarales brambles [I23]

jarcia rigging [II1]; —s harness [II5], equipment [II26]

jardín garden [I6]

jarro pitcher [I5]

jaspe jasper [I50]

jaspeado stained [II32]

jaspear to create a marbled effect [II31]

jaula cage [I46]

jayán giant [I5]

jazmín jasmine [II20]

jerigonza gibberish [I11]

jimia female ape [II39]

jineta, a la [saddle] with short stirrups [I36], on horseback [II16], **subir a la jineta** to mount a horse [I10]

jinete horseman [I41]

jira picnic [II28]

jirón pennant [II27], quality [II32]

jironado colorful triangular appliqués [II16]

¡jo! whoa [II10]

jocundo cheerful [II61]

jornada expedition, distance covered in a day [I29], military campaign [I39], journey [I41], act of play [I48], situation [II27]; **hacer** — to spend the night [I2]

jornalero day-laborer [I28]

joya jewel [I6], reward [I31]

jubilar to take pleasure [I37]

jubón doublet [I29]

judicial judicial [I45]

judío Jew [II8]

juego game [I4], gambling [II49]

juez judge [reI]

jugador player [II19]

jugar de manos sleight of hand [II27]

juglar troubadour [II31]

juguete toy [II62]

juguetón playful [I17]

juicio sanity [I1], judgment [dedI], crowd [II19]; **falto de** — out of one's wits [I13], — **temerario** rash judgment, **día del** — Judgement Day [II20]

jumenta female donkey [II10]

jumentil referring to **jumento** [II33]

jumento donkey [I5]

junco rush *botanical* [II20]

juntamente at the same time [I24], — **con** together with [reI], together [I41]

juntar to gather [I35], —**se** to join [I21], to make love [II48], to gather together [II58]

juntillas, a pies firmly [II52]

junto together [I4], close [I41], — **a, de** next to [I3], —**s** combined [I22]

juntura joining [II62]

jurado sworn [I4]; civil servant [I6]

juramento oath [prI]

jurar to swear [I8]

jurídicamente, proveer to put in legal form [II72]

juridición jurisdiction [priv. II]

jurisconsulto legal expert [II16]

jurisperito professor of law [II42]

justa joust [I49], contest [I16]

justamente justly [II30]

justicia justice [dedI], minister of justice [reI], authority [I48]

justiciar to condemn [I51]

justísimo very just [I34]

justo pious [I7], proper [I12], just [I18], tight [II60]; **al** — straightly [I10], just right [II36]

juzgado decided [I30], judgment [II1]

juzgar to judge [I4], to find [prI], to consider [II16]

L

laberinto labyrinth [I25]

labio lip [I13]

labor piece of work [I50], embroidery [II48], — **blanca** back-stitching [II48]

labrado embroidered [II20]

labrador,-a peasant [I1], farmer [II18]

labrandera seamstress[II48]

labranza farming [II9]

labrar to bring about [I33], to whittle [I41], to toil [II2], to embroider [II8], to build [II24], to make [II62]

lacayo groom [II31]

lacayuno pertaining to a groom [II56]

ladearse to swerve [I20]

ladito corner [II41]

lado side [I18], corner [I4]; **ir de medio** — to list [I8]

ladrido bark [pról. II], barking [II34]

ladrillazo blow with a brick [I25]

ladrillo brick [II20]

ladrón thief [prI]

lagañoso = legañoso bleary-eyed [II58]

lagar wine-press [I28]

lagartija lizard [I4]

lagartijero lizard-catching [II43]

lagarto lizard [I50]

lágrima tear [prI]

laguna lake [I29]

lambicar el cerbelo to wrack one's brains [II22]

lamentable lamentable [I31], moving [II16]

lamentación lamentation [I32]

lamentarse to lament [I51]

lamento lament [I23]

lamer to lick [II22]

lámpara lamp [II8]

lampazo green dock [I11]

lampiño beardless [II40]

lana wool [I7], de agua y — of little worth [II13]

lance episode [II13]

lancero man with lance [II58]

lanteja = lenteja lentil [I1]

lanterna = linterna lantern [I23], beacon [II53]

lanza lance [I1]

lanzada blow, thrust with lance [I8]

lanzar to shoot [II19], —se to throw oneself [II8]

lanzón metal-tipped stick [I17]

lapidario gem cutter [I33]

larga, a la extensively [I5]

largo long [prI], pasar de — to pass by [II16], de — a largo full length [II23]

lascivia lewdness [I48]

lascivo lustful [I11], lascivious [II51]

lastar to pay [II16]

lástima pity [I13], lamentation [I42]

lastimado doleful [I15], damaged [I31], hurt [II43], wounded [II44]

lastimar to injure [I20], to hurt [I28]

lastimero doleful [I42/43]

lastimoso doleful [I27], sad [I39]

lata, hoja de — tin [II12]

látigo whip [I4]

latín Latin [II29], mal — continuado mistake [II18]

latinico little Latin phrase [prI]

latino Latin scholar [I22], pertaining to Latin [II16]

latrocinio theft [II57]

laúd lute [II12]

laureado crowned with laurel [II18]

lauro laurel [I14]

lavatorio washing [II32]

lazada bow-knot [I20]

lazo knot [I14], noose [II19]

le it [reI]

leal loyal [I18]

lealtad loyalty [I33]

lecho bed [I2]

lechón suckling pig [II20]

lector reader [prI]

ledanía litany [I52]

leer reading [I1]

legal faithful [I20]

legalidad faithfulness [II60]

legalmente faithfully [II7]

legislador lawmaker [prI]

legítimamente legitimately [I2]
legítimo legitimate [I6]
lego secular [II13]
legua league (5573 meters) [I8]
leído well-read [prI]
lejía soap [II32]
lejos far [prI], **desde** — from afar [I3]
lencería linen goods [I23]
lengua tongue [I2], language [II2]
lenguaje speech [I2]
lenitivo laxative [I20]
leña firewood [I40]
leño wood [I42/43]
león lion [I18]
leonado lion-colored [I18], tan [I16]
leoncito little lion [II17]
leonero lion keeper [II17]
leonés from the kingdom of León [II12]
lesa majestad treason [pról. II]
letanía list [II43]
letor = lector reader [II8]
letra handwriting [I23], motto [I18], **al pie de la** — to the letter [I1], handwriting [I23]; **—s**
letra, cont'd. learning [prI], learning [I39]; **sin —s** uneducated [II49]
letrado reading [I32], man of letters [I37]
letura reading [I1]

levadas series [II71]
levadiza, puente drawbridge [I2]
levantado arisen [I7], lofty [I6], raised [II7], presumptuous [II50]; noble person [II32]
levantador concocter [II23]
levantar to pick up [I5], to raise [II3], **—se** to get up [I3]
Levante east [II64]
levar to weigh [anchor] [II29]
leve trifling [I2]
ley law [I2]
leyenda reading [Iprol], legend [prI], text [II4]
leyente reader [prI]
lezna shoemaker's awl [II23]
liar to tie [I5], to bind [I22]
libelo lampoon [II1]
liberal liberal [I31]
liberalidad liberality [I39]
libertad freedom [prI], scandal [II22], freeing [II25]
libertador liberator [I8]
libertar to free [I29]
libio Libyan [I14]
libra pound [II14]
libranza bill of exchange [I25]
librar to free [I8], to deliver [I20], to go free [I25], **—se** to go free [I3], — **bien** to get along with [I40]
libre free [I4], free person [I47], **hacer** — to free [prI]
librea uniform [I27], livery [II17]
libremente easily [I41]

librería library [I6]
librillo de memoria
  memorandum book [I23]
licencia permission [I4], consent
  [II8], university degree [II18],
  — **poética** poetic license [II70]
licenciadillo little **licenciado**
  [II1]
licenciado university graduate,
  master's degree level [I5]
licenciosamente licentiously
  [aprob. II]
lición = lección instruction [I27]
lícitamente legally [I44]
lícito lawful [I8], proper [I28]
licor liquid [I10]
lid *arch.* fight [I3]
liebre hare [I16]
lienzo piece of cloth [I40], linen
  [I23], curtain [I42/43]
liga strip [I27], confederation
  [I39], garter [I51]
ligado bound [I27]
ligadura binding [I20]
ligamiento tying [II29]
ligera, a la lightly [II24]
ligeramente swiftly [I8]
ligereza nimbleness [I3],
  swiftness [I34], fickleness [I51]
ligero swift [I8], light [I27],
  trifling [I33]
ligero swift [I41], loose [I51],
  nimble [II20], easy [II41], light
  [II44]
ligítimamente = legítimamente

legitimately [I8]
ligítimo = legítimo legitimate
  [I21]
lililí Arabic war cry [II61]
lima file [I41]
límiste fine cloth [II33]
limitado thrifty [II31], limited
  [II44]
límite limit [I36], border [II6]
limosna alms [I22]
limpiar to clean [I1], to scour [I2]
limpieza purity [I14], cleanliness
  [II4]
limpio clean [I3], in itself (in
  alcahuete limpio) [I22], **sacar
  en -** to make [something] out
  [I52], **no sacar en** — to get
  nothing out of [I26], **quedar en**
  — to be clear [II27]
limpísimo very clean [II47]
linaje lineage [I1], family [II16]
lince lynx
lindeza charm [prI], beautiful
  things [II20], **a las mil —s**
  uncommonly pretty [I21]
lindo beautiful [I5]
línea line [I20], — **recta** straight
  line [II26], — **equinocial**
  equator [II29]
lino flax [I25]
lío bundle [II46]
líquido liquid [I50]
lirio lily [I31]
lirón dormouse [II14]
lisión = lesión injury [II55]

liso smooth [I12]

lisonja flattery [II2]

lisonjear to flatter [II21]

lisonjero flattering [aprob. II]

lista list [II9]

listo diligent [I4], fast [I47], prepared [I51]

lisura smoothness [aprob. II]

litera litter [I19]

liviandad frivolity [I33]

liviano light [I11], slight [I45], frivolous [II44]

lizo thread [I47]

llaga wound [I3], tear [II34]

llagar to injure [II32]

llagado injured [I29]

llama flame [I24]

llamar to call [I4], —**se** to be named [I1], to knock [I42/43], —**se a engaño** to claim that one has been deceived [I46]

llana, a la simply [prI]

llaneza sincerity [I11], plainness [II26]

llano plain [I14], flat [II13], smooth [II41]; smoothly [II40], even [II62]; **a paso** — smoothly [I34], **afirmar el pie** — to behave [I6], **de** — **en llano** plainly [II64]

llanto crying [I14], lament [I41]

llanura plain [I18]

llave key [I6], — **maestra** master key [II46]

llegar to approach [I1], to place [I4], to collect [I7], —**se** to come [II41]

llenar to fill [prI]

lleno filled [prI], pregnant [I52], **de** — entirely [I9], **de lleno en** — head on [II56]

llevadero tolerable [II13]

llevado carried away [I1], attracted [I35]

llevar to carry [I2], to take away [I7], to lead [I41], to charge (money) [II25], to wear [II42], —**se** to take away [II11], — **yo de ventaja** to have in addition [I18], — **a uno en peso** to carry someone out [II62]

lloramico crying [II49]

llorar to cry [I4]

lloro weeping [I25]

llorón cry-baby [I1]

lloroso tearful [I12], watery [II47]

llover to rain [I3]

llovido rained [I30], **como llovidos** abundantly [II7]

loable praiseworthy [I34]

loado praised [I48]

loba she-wolf [I39]

lobo wolf [I14]

lóbrego lugubrious [II35]

Lobuna wolfish [II38]

loco crazy person [I1]; **volverse** — to go crazy [I42/42],

locura lunacy [I2], madness [I22]

lodo mud [I25]

logrado, mal unlucky [II23], ill-fated [II48]

lograrse, mal = malograrse to come to naught [I21]

loma little hill [I18]

lomo loin [I18], **—s** ribs [I16], back [II69]

longincuo remote [II29]

longísimo very long [II36]

longura length [II16]

lonja portico [II8]

loor praise [I52]

loriga mail armor [I10]

losa gravestone [I14]

lozanía lustiness [II11]

lucero evening star (Venus) [I25]

luchador wrestler [II19]

lucido distinguished [II21], magnificent [II26]

lúcido lucid [II1]

luciente shining [I2], **— imagin** zodiac sign [I46]

lucio sleek [I16]

lucir to shine [I50]

luego soon [I2], right now [I4], right then [prI], quickly [I34], **— luego** right now [I2], **— al punto** right now, immediately [I8], **— que** as soon as [I2], **— en continente** immediately [I21], **— al momento** right then [I40], **— cuando** as soon as [I41]

luengo *arch.* long [I1]

lueñe far-off [I29]

lugar place [prI], village [I1],

opportunity [I2], effect [II21], **dar — a** to give occasion, opportunity [I6]

lumbre light [I14]

luminar luminary [I12]

luminaria lantern [I42/43]

luna moon [I12]

lunar mole [I30]

lunes Monday [II25]

lusitano Portuguese [I49]

lustre splendor [aprob. II]

luto in black [I19]

luz light [prI], **— natural** intelligence [II53]

M

machacar = machucar to pound [I8], to crush [I18]

macho he-mule [I16], male of the species [II17]

machucar to bruise [I18]

machuelo mule [II35]

macilento wan [II3]

macizo solid [I50]

madama madame *Fr.* [II44]

madeja skein [II35]

madera wood [II39]

madero bar [I46]

madre river bank [I20]

madrina step-mother *Ital.* [II14]

madrugada early morning [I13]

madrugador person who rises early [I1]

madrugar to get up early in the

morning [I21]
madurado seasoned [II17]
maduro mature [prI], ripe [I41]
maese master [I1]
maestra, llave master key [II46]
maestre de campo regiment
    commander [I42]
maestresala steward [II31]
maestría skill [I18]
maestro doctor [I1], teacher [I25],
    judge [II19]
maga sorceress [II48]
magia magic [II14]
mágico magic [I30]
magín imagination [II3]
magnánimo heroic [I29]
magnificencia magnificence
    [I30]
magnífico generous [I13]
magnitud magnitude [II32]
Magno great [II2]
mago magician [II16]
magro meager [II33]
maguer although *arch.* [I25]
maguera although *arch. and
    rustic*[II33]
maherido prepared [II19]
Mahoma Mohammed [I18]
mahomético Muslim [II53]
majada hut [I2], sheep-fold [I11]
majadería foolish speech [I22]
majadero blockhead [I17]
majagranzas stupid bore [II31]
majar to pound [II6]
majestad majesty [I30], **su** — the

king [I22]
mal harm [I5], ill [prI], malady
    [I7], injury [I28]; scarcely [I7];
    evil [I22]; — **año** imprecation
    such as *heaven forbid!* or *too bad!*
    [I4], trouble [I4], — **de su grado**
    against one's wishes [I8]; —
    parado in bad shape [I22]; —
    que le pese however much it
    may displease you [I22]; —
    haya curses on [I34]
mala gana, de reluctantly [I22]
malandante unfortunate person
    [I19]
malandanza misfortune [I17]
malandrín brigand [I4]
malaventura misfortune [I13]
malaventurado unfortunate
    person [I22]
malbaratar to make a bad deal
    [I7]
maldad evil (thing) [I39],
    misdeed [II22]
maldecir(se) to curse (oneself)
    [I17]
maldiciente slanderer [prI],
    slandering [I33]
maldición curse [I27]
maldito damned [I5]
maleador trickster [II4]
maleante rogue [I2]
maleficio damage [I35]
malencólico = melanólico [II36]
malenconía = melancolía [I21]
malencónico = melancólico

melancholic [I22]
maleta valise [I23]
maletilla little valise [I32]
malévolo mischievous [II33]
malezas underbrush [I23]
malhadado ill-fated [I20]
malhechor evildoer [I42/43]
malicia wickedness [I11],
  badness [II13], malice [II26],
  mischievousness [II31], astute
  thing [II70]
malicioso malicious [I33],
  mischievous [I51]
maligno wicked (person) [I18],
  perverse [II10]
malísimo very bad [II71]
malla mail (armor) [II1]
malo devil [II61]
malparado in a sorry state [I45],
  wronged [I29]
malquisto detested [I11]
malsonante offensive [II59]
maltratado abused [I10]
maltratar to abuse [I15]
maltrecho ill-treated [I3]
malvado evil [II29]
mamar to suckle [II16]
mamona slap [II28]
maná (liquid) manna [II14]
manada herd [I2], flock [I4]
manantial spring [II18], running
  [II47]
manar to ooze [I4]
manceba mistress [I25]
mancebito very young man

[II24]
mancebo young man [II12]
mancha spot [I22], disgrace [I33]
manchada spotted [I50], "Spotty"
  [I50]
manchar to spatter [I21], to
  tarnish [I52]
manchego Manchegan [I2]
mancilla blemish [I52]
manco lacking [I9], one-armed
  person [II36], maimed in one
  arm [II44]
manda order [I26], bequest [II74]
mandadería *arch.* errand [I26]
mandado mandate [reI],
  command [I15]; sent [II10]
mandamiento order [I4],
  commandment [I29], warrant
  [I45]
mandar command [I2], to order
  [I2], to assure [I7], to promise
  [II10], to guarantee [II58], to
  assure [II70], to bequeath [II74]
manderecha luck [II22]
mando command [II51]
mandoble two-handed slash
  [II19]
manejar to work [II25]
manera way [prI], **de — que** so
  that [I1]
manga sleeve [I31], **de haldas o
  de —s** one way or another
  [II51]
manida lair [I24], **tener —** to
  have abode [I23]

manifestar to state [I12], to prove [I33], —**se** to show oneself [I34]

manifiestamente clearly [I29]

manifiesto clear [I13], **de** — exposed [I11], on display [II20]

manjar food [I10], — **blanco** creamed chicken breasts [II62]

mano power [I19], **en la** — obvious [II8], **de mano en** — handed down [I13], **a** — on hand [I15], **a dos** —**s** with both hands [I3], **si a** — **viene** perhaps [I42/43], **traer entre** —**s** to be working on [II18], **ir a la** — to cut off [II31], **a** — **salva** easily [II73]

manojo bunch [II61]

manosear to touch [I33], to rummage through [II3], to scrub [II32], to smooth [II36], to manhandle [II45]

manotadas, dar to paw [I20]

manquedad handicap [II51]

mansamente meekly [II11]

mansedumbre gentleness [I18]

manso meek [I15], gentle [I20]

manta mule blanket [I16], blanket [I17]

manteado blanketed [I20]

manteador blanketer [I17]

mantear to blanket [I17]

mantel tablecloth [I10]

mantellina shawl [I29]

mantenedor keeper [II18]

mantenerse to feed oneself [II13]

mantenido nourished [II47]

mantenimiento nourishment [II47]

mantequilla butter [II29]

mantilla diaper [I48]

manto cloak [prI], veil [II56]

mantón shawl [I50]

manual account book [I3]; manageable [I3]

manzana apple [I10]

maña dexterity [I10], astuteness [I39], custom [II39]

mañana tomorrow [I3], morning [I3]

mañero feasible [II1], meek [I7]

mañeruelo gentle [II73]

mañosamente skillfully [aprob. II]

mañoso clever [II48]

mapa map [II6]

maqinar to plot [I35]

máquina contrivance [prI], machine [I38], machinery [II62], multitude [I2], scheme [I25], sumptuous building [I8]

mar sea [prI]

maraña intrigue [II21]

maravedí 1/34 of a **real** [tasa I]

maravilla wonder [prI]

maravillado in awe [I23]

maravillar to astonish [I42], —**se** to marvel [I27], **no es de** — it's not surprising [II3]

maravillosamente marvelously [I9]

maravilloso marvelous [I14], admirable [I13]

marca, de más de la superior [I22]

marcar to designate [I16], to situate [I40]

marchar to march [I18]

marchitarse to wither [II22]

marchito faded [I18]

marcial warlike [II36]

marfil ivory [I13]

marfuz deceitful [I40]

margarita pearl [I34]

margen margin [prI], bank [I51]

marido husband [I2]

marina coast [I31], seashore [I40], shore [II63]

marinero sailor [I42/43]

marino marine [II58]

mármol marble [I2]

maroma rope [II55]

marqués marquis [dedI]

marquesa marquise [II48]

marras, de of yesteryear [I25]

marrido under the weather [II65]

Marruecos Morocco [II5]

marta (cebellina) sable [II14]

martillo hammer [I33]

martirio torture [II69]

martirizado tortured [I11]

mas but [I1], **mas que** although [I20]

más furthermore [reI], more so [I17], any longer [I34], greater [II8], especially [II37], ever again [II65], **sin — ni más** heedlessly [I7], without further ado [I19], **— a menos** more or less [I15], **— acá** on this side [I29], **— que** although [II20]

masa dough [II20], **— de mazapán** almond paste [II26]

mascar to chew [I11]

máscara mask [I19]

mástil mast [II1]

mata shrub [I23], bush [I21], sprig [II34]

matador killer [II47]

matalotaje provisions [I19]

matalote nag [II61]

matar to kill [prI], to put out (a flame) [I44]

matemáticas mathematics [II18]

materia matter [I2], topic [prI]

matizado harmonizing [II67]

matizar to stain [I34]

matorral thicket [I31]

matrimonio marriage [I12]

matrimoñesco of matrimony [I46]

matrona matron [II20]

mayar to meow [II9]; meowing [II46]

mayor greater [I1], greatest [prI], powerful [I22], chief [II23]; superior [I25]; **-es de marca** unique [II16]

mayoral overseer [I28], captain [II60]

mayorazgo great house (lineage)

[II24], principal heir [II54]

mayordomo superintendent [I28], steward [II36]

mayormente principally [dedI]

mazapán, masa de almond paste [II26]

mazmorra dungeon [I42], pit [II23]

mazo wooden hammer [I20], mass [I29]

mazorca cluster [II10]

meaja coin of little value [II2]

Meca, de Ceca en from one place to another [I18]

medalla image [II62]

medianamente moderately [I41]

medianero go-between [I13], mediator [I46]

mediano average [I48]

mediar to mediate [I46], to split the difference [II26]

medias stockings [I51]

medicina medicine [I11]

médico doctor [I52]

medida measurement [prI], **tomar la —** to measure [II3], **a la misma —** in kind [II58]

medido measured [I31]

medio half [I1], means [I33], **por — through the middle [I1], — cuerpo arriba** from the waist up [I4], **en —** between them

medir to weigh [I27], to measure [I33], **de —** measurable [II23]

medrado, estar splendid! [II47]

medrar to ger promoted [I38], to prosper [II14]

medrosico afraid [I16]

medroso fearful [I3]

mejilla cheek [prI]

mejora improvement [II50]

mejorar to make better [I2], **—se** to get better [pról. II]

mejoría improvement [I52]

melancólico sad person [prI]

melanconía = melancolía melancholy [I20]

melena lock of hair [II31]

melificado honeyed [I25]

melifluo honeyed [I2]

melindre prudery [I32], queasiness [I49], **—s** fussing [I1], amorous [II48]; **no hacer — not to be reluctant** [I40]

melindroso namby-pamby [I1], prudish [I12], priggish [I34], **a lo —** in an affected way [II62]

melón cantaloupe [II32]

membrarse de *arch.* to remember [I2]

membrudo burly [II14]

memorable memorable [II19]

memoria remembrance [I2], memory [I7]

memorial petition [II6]

memorioso with greatest memory [II12]

mención mention [II8]

mendigar to beg [prI]

mendigo beggar [II6]

mendrugo scrap [I10], crust (of bread) [II20]

menear(se) to stir [I5], to shake [I45], to manage lace bobbins [II6], to handle [II19]

meneo shaking [II45]

menester necessary [I2], need [I2]; function [I10]; duties [I31]

menesteroso needy [I3]

mengua discredit [I7], distress [I44]

menguado diminished [prI], wretched [II17], impaired [II41]; wretch [I52]

menguar to diminish [I11], to grow smaller [II5]

menjurje = mejunje cosmetics [II39]

menor least [I13], youngest [I39], lesser [II23]

menos lacking [II26], **a lo —** at least [prI], **echar —** to miss [I17]

menoscabar to impair [I11], to diminish [I11], to lessen [I27]

menoscabo discredit [I12], damage [I35]

menospreciado despised [I45]

menospreciar to scorn [II3]

menosprecio contempt [I20], scorn [II3]

mensajería errand [II10]

mensil monthly [II23]

mentar to mention [I21]

mentecatería nonsense [II32]

mentecato idiot [I37], half-wit [II16]

mentir to lie [I4]

mentira lie [prI], lying [I28], fiction [I47]

mentiroso deceitful [I6]; liar [I9]

mentís liar [I24], denial [II14]

menudamente in great detail [II17]

menudear to repeat [I8], to rain (blows, etc.) [I15]

menudencia trifle [I9]

menudo fine [I18], small [I31], thick [II19], low [II32], in a detailed way [II47]; **a —** frequently [I11], **por —** in detail [I48]

meo annual flowering plant [II29]

meollo understanding [I48]

meón constantly urinating [II29]

meramente merely [II13]

mercader merchant [I4], **hacer orejas de —** not to listen [II48]

mercadería commodity [I48]

mercaduría merchandise [II19]

mercancía business [I39], cargo [I40

merced favor [I3], pleasure [reI], gift [II8], mercy [II15], **— a** thanks to [II36]; **vuestra —** your grace = you [I1], **vuesa —** your grace *rustic*, **su —** *ironic* him [I6], **— a** thanks to [I24], **a mercedes** by favors [II7]

merecedor deserving [I1]
merecer to deserve [I1]
merecido deserved [I24]
merecimiento merit [I1]
merendar to eat lunch [II22]
méritamente deservedly [II3]
mérito merit [I21]
mero mere [II16], alone [II18]
mes month [I16]
mesarse to tear out [I41]
mesmo = **mismo** same [I1],
  him/herself [I41], itself [II29]
mesnada followers [II21]
mesón inn [I17]
mesura politeness [I2], **hacer —**
  to bow [II64]
metad = **mitad** middle [II58]
metáfora metaphor [II22]
metal metal [I40]
metamorfóseos transformation
  [I37]
meter to put [I7], **—se** to be
  concerned with [II19], to
  become [II40]
metro verse [II4]
mezcla mixture [prI]
mezclado mixed [I11]
mezclar to mix [prI]
mezquino stingy [I39], wretched
  [II10]
mezquita mosque [II26]
micer my lord [I49]
miedo fear [I2]
miel honey [II20], **de —es** sweet
  [I32]

miembro limb [I18]
mientes mind [I52], thoughts
  [I4], **tener — en** to think about
  [I42/43]
migaja nothing [II50]
migas rustic stew [I22]
mil one thousand [I5]
milagro miracle [prI], **a —**
  miraculous [I23]
milagrosamente miraculously
  [II18]
milagroso miraculous [I33]
milano kite (bird) [II22]
milesio milesian [I47]
milicia military [I45]
militar to go to war [I18]
milla mile "1000 steps" [I4]
millar thousand [II6]
millón million [I26]
mina mine [I6]
minar to tunnel through [I34], to
  tunnel [I38], to mine [I40]
mínima half-note [= slightest
  thing] [I31]
mínimo smallest [I16], minimal
  [I14]
ministerio capacity [I11]
ministro servant [I11], minister
  [I13]
mira sight [prI], **a la —** on the
  lookout [II2]
mirada way of looking at things
  [II41]
mirado thought of [I33], **mal —**
  uncouth [I47], **bien —** well

mannered [II6]

mirador battlement [II26]

mirante gazing [II56]

mirar to look at [prI], to consider [I4], to notice [I11], to find [I41], to glance [I25], to pay attention [II6]; — **a** to care about [I35], — **de hito en hito** to stare [I28], — **por** to look after [II4], — **en** to pay attention [II34], to notice [II50]

mirón onlooker [II49]

mirto myrtle [II34]

misa mass [I26]

miserable wretched [I13], stingy [I39], **de** — out of stinginess [I4]; wretch [I22]

miseria misery [I15], pittance [II60]

misericordia mercy [I6], "praise" [I6], compassion [II1], drop [II33]

misericordioso merciful [II3]

mísero wretched [I14]

mismísimo very own [I35]

mismo itself [I45]

misterio mystery [I6]

mistura compound [I22]

mitad half [I2], **por** — in half [I1], **en la** — in the middle [I8]

mitigar alleviate [I19]

mitra bishop's liturgical headdress [II7], hat [II69]

mocedad youth [I3], inexperience [II28]

mochacha = muchacha girl [II5]

mochacho = muchacho boy [II62]

mocho butt of rifle [II60]

mocoso puerile [II18]

moderar to lower [II25], to adjust [I26]

modo way [prI], manner [I33]

moharracho clown [II11], tramp [II54]

mohatra fraudulent [II31]

mohinísimo very mournful [I22]

mohino mournful [I4], annoyed [II26], angry [II32]

moho mildew [I1], rust [I49]

mojado wet [I25]

mojar to dip [II20]

mojicón blow to the face with a closed fist [I35]

mojón landmark [I25], connoisseur/taster of wines [II13]

molde, venir de to be just right [I4], to fit the circumstance perfectly [II1]

moldes set type [reI]

moledor assailant [I52]

moler to pound [I4]

molestia bother [I23]

molesto tiresome [aprob. II]

molido beaten-up [I4]

moliente y corriente perfect [II13]

molificar to soften [II38]

molimiento pounding [I5], fatigue [II44]

molinero miller [I3]

molino mill [I2], — **de viento** windmill [I2], **rueda de** — millstone [I32]

mollera top of the head [I7]

momento consequence [prI], moment [I41], importance [II58], **al** — right then [I4], **por —s** at any moment [I49]

momia, carne mummy [I50], **de** — mummified [II23]

mona monkey [II62]

mona: tomar la — to get drunk [II26], **hacer —s** to deceive [II27]

monacillo acolyte [II25]

monarca monarch [I21]

monarquía monarchy [I38]

monasterio monastery [II60]

mondar to pick teeth [I50], to trim [II40]

mondo pure [prI], plain [II5], gnawed [II54]

moneda money [I40], currency [II68]

monesterio = monasterio monastery [I35]

monísimo supreme monkey [II26]

monja nun [I35]

monjil nun's habit [II37]

monjío becoming a nun [I36]

mono monkey [II25]

monstro = monstruo monster [I14]

monta important thing [I34]

montante broadsword [I32]

montañés from the region of Santander [II48]

montañuela small mountain [I19], hill [I23]

montar to amount to [I4]

montaraz wild [I25]

¡montas! upon my faith [I21]

montazgo tribute [I22]

monte forest [I14], mount [I20], mountain [II20]

montera cap

montería, caza de big game hunting [II34]

montero beater in hunting [II34]

montiña forest [I5]

montón mound [I6], heap [I52], **a montones** lots of [II5]

montoncillo pile [I23]

morada dwelling place [I14]

morado purple [II23]

moralmente morally [I40]

morar to live [I24]

morbidez smoothness [II39]

morbo gálico syphilis [II22]

mordaza gag [II27]

morder to bite [prI]

morena "trouble" [I26]

moreno brown [II31], dark complected [II60]

morillo little Moor [I26]

morir to end [prI], to die [I5]

morisco Moorish [I37], Moorish language = Arabic [I41]

morisma multitude of Moors [II26]

moro Moor [I5], **a lo —** in the Moorish style [II26]

morrión open helmet [I1]

mortaja shroud [I14]

mortal able to kill [I14], mortal [II8]

mortífero deadly [II70]

mosca fly [I29]

mosén sir [I49]

mosquear to swat [II60]

mosqueo fly swat [II35]

mosquito gnat [I18]

mostaza mustard [II41]

mostrar to show [I7], to teach [I40], to pretend [I20], **—se** to appear [I20]

mostrenco vagabond [II2], ignorant [II51]

mota speck [II43]

mote motto [I18]

motilón lay brother [I25]

mover to move [I13]; **—se** to induce oneself [prI], to move [I8]

movible changeable [II14], mobile [II37], moveable [II41]

movimiento movement [I42/43], emotion [II68], **primeros —s** first impulses [I20]

moza lass [I1]

mozo young [I2], childish [I49]; lad [I1], servant [I15], **— de mulas** muleteer [I42], **— de**

caballos stable boy [I47]

mozuela young girl [II50]

muceta short cape [II54]

muchacha girl [I12]

muchacherías nonsense [II28]

muchacho boy [I3]

muchedumbre multitude [I14]

mucho very [I4], **no es —** it's no wonder [II16]

mudable changeable [I18]

mudamiento change [I34]

mudanza change [I8], dance figure [II20]

mudar to change [I1], **—se** to change [I7], to relieve oneself [I20], **— un paso** to take one step [II5]

mudas makeup [I20]

mudo dumb [I25], dumb person [I1], silent [II20]

muebles goods [I12]

mueca grin [I25]

muela molar [I18], tooth [I29]

muelle effeminate [II2]

muerte death [prI]

muerto dead [I2], killed [I5]

muestra sign [I2], indication [I14], proof [I39], demonstration [II22], appearance [II69]

mugre rust [II18]

mugriento grimy [I2]

mujer woman [I1], wife [I7], **—del partido** traveling prostitute [I2]

mujercilla silly woman [I22]
mujeriega: a la side-saddle [I23],
    a mujeriegas woman-style
    [I27]
mujeriego woman chaser [II51]
mula mule [I27]
muladar dung heap [II16]
muleta crutch [II8]
mulo mule [I3]
mundo world [prI]
muñeca wrist [I16]
muñido prepared [II19]
muñidor summoner [I21]
mur *Lat.* mouse [II56]
muralla wall [I39]
murar to wall up [I7]
murciélago bat [II22]
murmuración gossip [II42]
murmurador gossip [I46]
murmurar murmuring [prI]; to
    backbite [prI], to murmur
    [I29], to criticize [I3], —**se** to
    gossip [I12]
muro wall [prI]
musa muse [prI]
musaraña cobweb [II33]
músculo muscle [I42/43]
música music [I2]
músico musical [I1]; musician
    [I11]
muslo thigh [I20]
mustio sad [II54]
mutación transformation [II24]

N

nabo turnip [I35]
nace, de donde hence [II5]
nacer to be born [II27]
nacido born [I3]
nacimiento head (of river) [prI],
    birth [I6]
nación birth [I18], race [I9],
    nation [I33]
nadar to swim [I35]
nadie anyone [I20]
naipes playing cards [II24]
naranja orange [II8]
naranjo orange tree [I32]
narices nostrils [I9], nose [I26]
narigante nosed [II14]
narigudo big-nosed person [II14]
nariz nose [II14], — **roma** flat
    nose [I16]
narración account [I5]
nascer = **nacer** to be born [prI]
nata cream [I29]
natural born in [I3], native [I1],
    whole [II58]; bastard [I39],
    instinct [I41], naturalist [I33]; **al**
    — naturally [I29], **de (mi)** — by
    nature [II60]
naturaleza nature [prI], Nature
    [I14]
naufragio shipwreck [I47]
náusea nausea [ded. II]
navaja razor [I18]
navegar to navigate [I14], to go to
    sea [I39], to sail [II63]

navío ship [I34]
necedad foolishness [I5]
necesidad need [prI]
necesitado needed [prI], needful [I28], needy [II55]
neciamente foolishly [I34]
necio foolish [I25]
negar to deny [I4]
negociante negotiator [I46], with business to discuss [II47]
negociar to conduct business [II47]
negocio matter [I9], plan [I25], affair [I44]
negra fencing foil [II19]
negregura = negrura blackness [I50]
negro cursed [I3], black [I13]
negrura blackness [II36]
neguijón cavity [I18]
nervio nerve [I42/43]
nervoso sinewy [II23]
netezuelo, tercero great grandchild [II42]
ni por pienso absolutely not [I4]
nieto grandson [I13]
nieve snow [I13]
nigromancia black magic [I47]
nigromante magician [I31]
ninfa nymph [I26]
niña girl [II38], —s de los ojos eyeballs [II11]
niñería childish action [I8], trifle [I27]
niñez childhood [II41]

niño child [II13], — de la doctrina orphan [II35]
níspero crabapple-like fruit [II59]
nivelado balanced [II17]
no sé que, un a bit [I24]
noble noble [I37]
nobleza nobility [I21]
nocivo injurious [II47]
nombrado renowned [I4], appointed [reI]
nombrar to name [prI], to be named [I18], to mention [II3], to call [II33], to call by name [II62]
nombre renown [I1], name [I1], reputation [prI], price [I41], noun [II18]
non *arch.* no [I2]
nonada nothing [II6]
nones no's [I22]
norabuena = enhorabuena intensification word, no translation [II53]; **vaya** — go
norabuena, cont'd. your way [I22]
norte north star [I25]
notable notable [I34]
notar to notice [I23], to reprehend [I20], to dictate [II36], to note [II45]
noticia information [prI], knowledge [I15]
notificar to announce [I31]
notomía dissection [I34], anatomy [II11], skeleton [II35]

notorio evident [I4], notorious [I52]

noturno nocturnal [II22]

novedad uprising [I15], novelty [I42], news [I50]

novel novice [I2]

novela story [I32]

noventa ninety [I52]

novia bride [II19]

noviciado penitence [II66]

novillo bullock [II20]

nube cloud [I3]

nuca (del celebro) back of neck [II28]

nudo lump [I27], knot [I27]

nueva(s) news [I18]

nueve nine [I52]

nuevo new [prI], unusual [II69], **de —** again [I1], for the first time [I13]

nuez walnut [II13]

nunca never [I2]

ñudo = nudo knot [I2]

O

obedecer to obey [I2]

obedicido = obedecido obeyed [I8]

obediencia submission [I31], obedience [I28]

obispo bishop [prI]

objeción objection [II3]

obligación obligation [I40]

obligadísimo very obliged [I17]

obligado compelled [I24], obliged [I3]

obligar to compel [I5], to oblige [I24]; **—se** to promise [I49]

obra work [dedI], task [I13], deed [I37], **a — de** about [I8], **buena — good deed** [I20]; **poner por — to try, to put into effect** [I40]; **por la — in due course** [I46], **—s naturales** natural functions [I49]

obrar to act [I18], to perform [I30], to do [I40]

obsceno obscene [II59]

obsequias funeral dirges [I14]

observancia attention [I48]

obstante, no in spite of [II3]

ocasión risk [I1], reason [I4], opportunity [I2], cause [I13], excuse [I33], occasion [I16]

océano ocean [prI]

ocho días one week [I39]

ocio idleness [II26]

ociosidad idleness [I28]

ocioso idle [I1]

ocultar to hide [I47]

oculto concealed [I17], hidden [I45]

ocupado busy [I48]

ocupar to disturb [I29], to occupy [II41]

odio hatred [I39]

odioso detestable [aprob. II]

ofender to attack[I3], to harm [I6], to offend [I8], to take offensive action [I15], to bother [II19]

ofensa insult [I27]

ofensivo offensive [II16]

oficial workman [II49], artisan [II52]

oficina breeding place [I39], workshop [II43]

oficio occupation [I4], profession [II4]

oficioso obliging [II6]

ofrecer to offer [prI], —**se** to present oneself [I23], to come up [II7]

ofreciere, se me it occurs to me [I33]

ofrecimiento offering [I8], offer [I11]

ofrenda offering [II8]

ofuscar to blind [I35]

oídas, de by hearsay [I34]

oído heard [I7]; (inner) ear [I9], listener [II38]

oidor judge [I42]

oíslo *colloq.* wife [I7]

ojeado frightened [II58]

ojear to drive an animal [I33]

ojeo beating to drive animals [II58]

ojera rings under eyes [II23]

ojeriza ill-will [I7], dislike [I47], grudge [II1]

ojo eye [II19], **hacer del** — to wink [I22], **niñas de los** —**s** eyeballs [II11], **a** —**s vistas**

with his own eyes [II22]

ola wave [II1]

oler to smell [I15], suspect [II10]

olfato smell [I20], sense of smell [I49]

oliscar to smell [II40]

oliva olive tree [I14]

olivífero olive-bearing [I18]

olla stew [I1], pot [I17], **- de Egipto** high living [I22], — **podrida** stew [II47]

olmo elm tree [I22]

olor aroma [I11], smell [II16]

olorcillo little smell [I31]

oloroso fragrant [I50]

olvidado forgotten person [II22]

olvidar to forget [prI], —**se de** to forget [I2]

olvido oblivion [prI]

omecillo dispute [I10], hatred [I20]

omnipotente omnipotent [I46]

onza ounce [prI]

opinión view [prI], opinion [I37]

oponer a to compare [II54], —**se** to oppose [I28]

opresión pressure [I19]

opreso oppressed [I22]

oprimido oppressed [II29]

oprimir to press [I18]

oprobrio infamy [I34]

opuesto adverse [I7], contrary [II22]

ora or [I4], whether [I15], **ora…** — either… or [I24]

oración prayer [I3], speech [prI], sentence [prI]
oráculo oracle [I34]
orador speaker [I47]
oratoria art of oratory [I47]
oratorio chapel [II49]
orbe world [I46]
orden order [prI], plan [I40]
ordenado ordained [I7], ordered [I22]
ordenanza law [I44], order [II66]
ordenar to order [I13], to arrange [I33]
ordeñar to milk [II16]
ordinario usual [I5], accustomed [I19]; **de —** commonly [I1], usually [II51]
orearse to air oneself [II24]
oreja ear [prI]
orfandad orphanhood [I30]
órgano organ [II55]
orgullo pride [I39]
orgulloso proud [I19]
oriental oriental [II13]
Oriente East [I13]
origen origin [I6]
original original manuscript [reI]
orilla border [II11]
orín rust [I1]
orina urine [I22]
ornamento adornment [dedI]
oro gold [prI], **— bajo** gold alloy [I40]
orondo pot-bellied [II20], puffed up [II52]

oropel tinsel [I51], foil [II12]
orza, a luffing [I41]
osado daring [I49]
osar to dare [dedI]
ostentación vanity [I28], exaltation [II6]
ostugo corner [II9], nothing at all [I54]
otoño autumn [II53]
otorgar to grant [I3]
otra vez again [I4]
otro día the next day [I5]
oveja sheep [I4]
ovejuno of sheep [I31]
oviese = *arch.* **hubiese** [I29]
ovillo ball of yarn [I4]
oyas = **oigas** hear [I18]
oyente listener [I27]
oyo = **oigo** [I32]
o... o either... or [II41]

P

pacer to graze [I15], to eat [II10]
paciencia patience [I6], **llevar en — ** to tolerate [I25]
paciente patient [I50]
pacíficamente peacefully [I31]
pacífico mild [I2], tranquil [I7], peaceful [II20]
pacto pact [II15]
padecer to suffer [I2]
padrastro stepfather [prI], bad father [I39]
padrino best man [I27], second

(in duel) [II14]

padrón column with inscription [II39]

paga pay [I9], payment [I4]

pagado satisfied [I4], paid for [II17]

pagador payer [II14]

pagano pagan [I18]

pagar to pay [I4], to respond [I16], to make amends [I7], to repay [I17]

pago payment [I3], recompense [I13]

paja straw [I3], **en dacá las —s** in the twinkling of an eye [II18]

pajar hayloft [I16]

pajarica little bird [II59]

pajarillo little bird [I2]

pájaro bird [II12]

paje page [I26], **estudiantado —** page serving a student [I2]

pajecillo little page [I22]

pala shovel [II20], bat [II70]

palabra word [I16]; **de —** orally [I31], by messenger [I34]

palaciego of the court [II21]

palacio palace [I21]

paladar palate [II13]

paladino = paladín champion [I52]

paladión Palladium, erroneous name for the Trojan horse [II41]

palafrén woman's horse [I29], tame horse [I9]

palafrenero stable boy [II31]

palamenta banks of oars [II63]

paletas, en dos in an instant [II51]

palillo bobbin [II6], **— de dientes** toothpick [II6]

paliza beating [I15]

palma palm [I14], palm of the hand [I18]

palmada slap [prI]

palmadica little slap [I25]

palmadita little slap [pról. II]

palmilla fancy cloth [II20]

palmito, como un with lots of clothing [II5]

palmo span, 8 inches I16]

palo blow [I4]; wood [I15], stick [I16], rod [II43]

paloma dove [I46]

palomar pigeon house [II7]

palomino young pigeon [I1]

palpable palpable [I33]

palpar to feel [I47]

pan bread [I2], loaf of bread [I52], **pan —** bread with added olive oil and sesame seed [I17]

pandero tambourine [II19]

panecillo bread roll [II67]

panegírico poet [II70]

paniaguado protégé [I52], servant [I13]

pantalia soot [II44]

pantuflo slipper [I1]

panza belly [I23]

pañales shirttails [I25]

pañizuelo handkerchief [I23]
paño cloth [I28], **— de tocar** kerchief [I28], **de** woven [I27], **— de cabeza** night cap [I17]
papa pope [II13]
papahigo winter cap [II50]
papar to eat *colloq.* [I18], **— viento** to waste time [II31]
papel paper [I8], role [II11]
papelón cardboard [I2]
papesa = papisa female pope [II50]
papilla deception [I32]
papirotazo whack [II70]
par pair [I4], peer [I5], **de par en — wide** open [I14], **al — de** equally [I8]
parabién felicitation [I33]
parada bet (in cards) [II35]
paradero stopping place [I13], end [II6]
parado standing there [I23], **tal han — in** such a state [I5], **mal — badly** battered [I15]
paraíso paradise [I42]
paraje place [I41]
paramento caparison [II34], **figura de — knick-knack** [II5]
páramo desert [I14]
paranza hunting blind [II34]
parapoco numbskull [II62]
parar to end [I4], to end up [I42], to stop [I18], to leave [I31], **—se** to stop [I4], to wind up [I9]

parasismo = paroxismo loss of consciousness [I17]
parcas fates [II38]
parche patch [II25]
parcialidad group [II21]
pardiez by God [I36]
pardo dark grey [I21]
parecer to show [I3], to appear [I2], to seem [prI]; judgment [I21], advice, **a mi — in** my opinion [prI]; **buen — good** looks [I1], **mal — bad** looks [I17], **al — seemingly** [I13]
parecido similar [II6], shown up [II25]
pared wall [I5], **— y media** next door [II16]
pareja mate [II19], **correr —s** to match [prelim.I]
parentela ancestry [I21], kinfolk [I22]
pares even numbers [II53]
parido given birth [I9]
pariente relative [prI]
parir to give birth
párpado eyelid [II53]
parsimonia moderation [II62]
parte cause [I4], share [I13], place [I21], quality [I49], trait [II13], source [II33], accuser [II56]; **—s** places [II51], circumstances [II66]; **de mi — on** my part [I40], **por esta — on** this account [I4], **dar — to** inform [I2], **esta — around** here [prI], **a**

una — somewhere [I18], aside [II18], **por** — where [I34], **por — de** on the side of [II13], endowments [I24], qualities [I27], **buenas** — good looks [I33], **todas** — everywhere [I2], — **segunda** understudy [I32], **ninguna** — nowhere [I36], **de parte a** — asunder [II56]

partesana large halberd [II27]

participar to participate [II3]

particular personal [I14], private [I37], indivual [I40], particular [II19], case [II31], **en** — extraordinarily [II65]

particularidad, cosas de details [I30]

particularmente particularly [I44]

partida departure [I21], item [II42], match [II71]

partido split [I1], divided [I18], advantage [I11]; **a brazo** — onm equal terms [II60], **mujeres del** — traveling prostitutes [I2]

partir to split [I1], to share [I3], —**se** to leave [I7]

parto birth [prI]

parva unthreshed corn [II68]

pasa raisin [I9]

pasada, de in passing [II72]

pasado transgressed [I15], happened [I4], past [II8], forebear [II57]

pasagonzalo slap to the nose [II14]

pasaje crossing [II51]

pasajero well-traveled [I8], transient [I8], traveler [I32]

pasamanos trim [II46]

pasar to be past [I1], to happen [I2], to pierce [I12], to spend time [I15], to suffer [I15], to take [I20], to stab [I34], to live [I2], to speak [II7], to do [II7], to escape [II10]; — **adelante** to proceed [I27]; —**se** to go over [I20], — **de** to surpass [I17], **de — a parte** run through [I4], — **en blanco** to miss [I16], — **de la memoria** to forget [I19], — **mal** to have a bad time of it [I22], — **adelante** to continue [I15], — **de largo** to pass by [II16], — **la tela** to enter the contests [II17]

pasatiempo amusement [I6]

Pascua Easter [I31]

pasear to walk [I3], to slide [II29], —**se** to stroll [II19]

paseo walk [I3]

pasión passion [I4]

pasitamente quietly [II41]

pasito quietly [I29]; careful [II30

pasmado stunned [II14]

pasmar to stun [II10], —**se** to be stunned [I19], to be stupified [I20]

pasmo astonishment [II55]

paso encounter [I4], challenge [I4], step [I4], situation [I4], passage [I5], pace [I18], incident [I27], slowly [II62], strait [II63]; in a low voice [II49];, **dar un —** to take a step [I8], **buen —** easy life [I13], **de — briefly [I27]; a cada —** all the time [I31], at every turn [I40]; **a — llano** smoothly [I34], **a — tirado** at a brisk pace [I10], **pasito a —** one step at a time [II26]

pasta, de buena fool [II52]

pasto pasture [I18]

pastor shepherd [prl]

pastoral relating to shepherds [I51]

pata foot (of animal) [I20], **—s arriba** head over heels [I20], dead [II43]

patada stamp with foot [I46]

patán hayseed [II47]

patear to trample [I45]

patente patent [I48]; obvious [II4]; **hacer —** to reveal [II36]

patentemente clearly [II35]

paternidad paternity [I47]

paternostre the Our Father prayer [I17]

patio patio [I3]

patochada stupid thing [II7]

patraña fabulous story [I25]

patria place of birth [I1], country [I1]

patriarca patriarch [I7]

patrón master [I39]

pavés body-length shield [II53]

pavor fear [II21]

paz peace [I8]; **dar —** to kiss [I42/43], **hacer las paces** to make peace [I46], **por bien de — for** a little peace [I20]

pazpuerca foul woman [II5]

peana litter [I52], pedestal [II5]

pecado sin [I1]; sinned [I33]

pecador,-a sinner [I5]

pecar to sin [I42/43]

pechero commoner [I15]

pecho chest [I4], heart [I3], bosom [I11], tribute [I45], **buen — goodness** of heart [II8], **mal — ill-will** [II57], **desembarazar el —** to clear one's throat [II12]

pectición petition [II72]

pedagogo tutor [I15]

pedazo piece [I1], **hecho —s** broken to bits [I5]

pedernal flint [II44]

pedernalino hard [II35]

pedestre ordinary [II66]

pedimiento petition [tasa II]

pedir to demand [I4], to ask for [tasa II], **— prestado** to borrow [I7], **a — de boca** perfectly [II62]

pedrada blow with stone [prl]

pedreñal flint pistol [II60]

pedrezuela little stone [I50]

pedrisco shower of stones [I22]

pegadizo contagious [I6], attachable [II44]

pegado attached to [I17], laid on [II35]

pegajoso viscous [II13], sticky [II40]

pegar to stick on [I29], to stick [II12], — **fuego** to set fire [I6], — **el ojo** to close one's eyes [II23]

pegote sticky patch [II40]

pegujar parcel of land [II2]

peinarse to comb [I31]

peine comb [I20]

peje fish [II18]

peladilla pebble [I18]

pelado plucked [I7], hairless [I35], smooth [I14]

pelaje dressed [I52]

pelar to shear [I22], to tear out [II1]

pelaza scuffle [I16]

pelea fight [I16]

peleante combattant [II14]

pelear fighting [I2]; to fight [I7]

peligro danger [I1], peril [I42/43]

peligrosísimo very dangerous [I19]

peligroso dangerous [I8]

pella cake [II32]

pellejo skin [II20]

pellico shepherd's jacket [I12]

pellizcar to pinch [II48]

pellizco pinch [II69]

pelo hair [I8], pile [II21], **venir a**

— to suit perfectly [prI]

pelón worthless person [II24]

pelota ball [I32], **en** — entirely naked [I15], without a coat [II54]

peludo hairy [II23]

pena punishment [I6], sorrow [I14], grief [I20], penance [I25], torment [II55], **so** — under penalty [reI], **no tener** — not to worry [I10], **a duras** —**s** with great difficulty [I21], **en** — in torment [II48]

penado laborious [I17]

penar to agonize [I8]

pendencia quarrel [I1], fight [I21]

pender to hang [II38]

pendiente hanging [I8], in suspense [II26]

péndola pen [I22]

penitencia penance [I10], **hacer** — to take pot-luck [II3]

penitenciado condemned person [II69]

penosamente in pain [II28]

pensado deliberate [I50], **no** — unexpected [I47]

pensamiento thought [prI], resolution [I13], plan [II64], **ni por** — absolutely not [I23]

pensar to devise [I33], to plan [prI], to imagine [I2], to feed [II20]

pensativo worried [I5], pensive [I18]

penuria poverty [prI]
peña large rock [I2], boulder [I11]
peñasco large rock [I128]
péñola quill pen [II74]
peñón rocky cliff [I25]
peón hod carrier [I20]
pepita pip (a chicken's throat disease) [II5]
pequeñez smallness [II45]
pera pear [I22]
peraile = **pelaire** wool carder [I17]
percebir to comprehend [II55]
percibir to comprehend [I28]
perder: — **el juicio** to go crazy [I1], — **los estribos** to talk nonsense [I49], **echar a** — to ruin [II26]
perdía = **perdería** [I33]
perdición ruin [I22], death [II29]
pérdida loss [I33]; lost soul [II48]
perdido lost [I33]
perdidoso having-lost [II25]
perdigón partridge [II16]
perdiz partridge [II43]
perdón pardon [I2]
perdonar to pardon [prI], to forgive [I17]
perecer to die [I19], to perish [I20]
peregrinación wandering [II12], pilgrimage [II25]
peregrinar to roam [II2]
peregrino rare [I1], exotic [I42-43]

pereza laziness [prI], sloth [II8]
perezosamente lazily [I33]
perezoso lazy [prI]
perfeción perfection [I25]
perfeta = **perfecta** [I33]
perfetísimo most perfect [II16]
perficionar to perfect *Latinized form* [II16]
perfumado perfumed [I50]
pergamino parchment [I45]
pergenio intention [I21]
pericto = **perito** experienced [I47], expert [II16]
período sentence [prI]
perito qualified [II16]
perjudicar to harm [II16]
perjudicial harmful [I14], prejudicial [II12]
perjuicio detriment [I4]
perla pearl [I1], **de** —**s** perfectly [I31]
permitiese to permit [I49]
pero however [I52]
perpetuo perpetual [I6]
perplejo perplexing [II11], perplexed [II64]
perrico,-a dog [II25]
perrilla dog [II25]
perrita dog [II68]
perro dog [I23]
perroquia = **parroquia** parish [I27]
perseguimiento persecution [II48]

perseguir to pursue [I16], to attack [pról. II]

perseverar to persevere [I10]

persona, en in person [II11]

personaje personage [prI], character [I34]

personilla little person [II43]

persuadiendo inducing [I22]

persuadir to persuade [I7]

persuasión persuasion [II12]

pertenecer to pertain [I10]

perteneciente pertinent [II1], appropriate [II59]

pertinacia stubbornness [II46]

pertinaz obstinate [14]

pertrechar to repair [I7]

pertrechos weaponry [I2], munitions [I34]

perturbar to disturb [I25]

perverso perverse [II16]

pesadilla nightmare [I16]

pesado heavy [I8], offensive [I23], — **sueño** deep sleep [I42]

pesadumbre unpleasantness [I7], boredom [I13], gravity [I8], grief [I9], weight [I50], **dar** — to bother [I6]

pésame condolence [I14]

pesar grief [II26]; to displease [I17], to grieve [I34], **mal que le pese** however much it may displease you [I22]; grief [I12], **a — de** in spite of [I6]

pesaroso sorrowful [I8]

pescado fish [I2]

pescador fisherman [II29]

pescar to fish [II13], to search [I29]

pescozada slap on the neck [I3]

pescuezo neck [II12]

pesebre manger [II24]

pésete curse [I15]

pesia a mí for God's sake [I17]

pésimo very bad [II33]

peso weight [I2], **en** — bodily [II69]

pespetiva = perspective appearance [II14]

pesquería fishery [I39]

pestaña eyelash [I23]

pestífero noxious [II32]

pestilencia plague [I11], foul [II41]

pestilente foul [I19]

peto breastplate

petral horse's front strap [II20]

pez *f* pitch [I50]

piadoso merciful [I12], pious [I25]

piara herd of swine [II68]

pica pike [II27]

picada pecked [I23]

picado irate [I4], rough [I41]

picante, no nada not amusing [II62]

picar to spur [I4], to nibble [II22]. to sting [II67], **—se** to pride oneself [II19]

pícaro mischievous [II62], — **de cocina** kitchen boy [II32]

pichón pigeon [II3]

pico sharp point [I16], pick-axe [I13], tip [I21], **poner en —** to tell [II50]

picota gallows [II49], pillory [II52]

picote coarse material made of goat hair [II69]

píctima medicinal plaster [II58]

pidir = pedir to ask for [II45]

pie foot [I3], **a —** on foot [I7], **en — ** standing up [II25], whole [II70], **a - quedo** without taking a step [II6], **al — de** about [I23], **— de altar** altar fees [I26], **— -de-amigo** iron collar [I22], **levantarse en —** to stand up [II18], **al — de la letra** to the letter [I1]

piedra stone [I3], jewel [I33], **— del molino** millstone [I8]

piel skin [II11], fur [I33]

piélago high sea [I34]

pienso feed [II5], **ni por —** absolutely not [I4]

pierna leg [I19], **a — tendida** stretched out [II9]

pieza coin [I2], head (of cattle, etc.) [I2], distance [I4], time [I7], fragment [I21], piece [I41]

pífaro fife [II34]

pila stone trough [I3]

piloto navigator [I34]

pincel brush [II32]

pinganitos, en prosperous [I47]

pino pine wood [I15], **— de oro** very charming [II50]

pintado colored [I2], best [I3], painted [II6], **como el más —** like the best of them [II19]

pintar to describe [I23], to paint [prI], **—se** to be described [I2], to be painted [I2]

pintiparado perfectly like [I21], perfectly [I44]

pintor painter [prI]

pintura painting [II46]

pío pious [II74]

piojo louse [II29]

piojoso lousy [I13]

pipote little barrel [I26]

pique: a — in danger [I22], on the point of [I29], liable [II27] **cuan —** with what ease [I11]

pirámide pyramid [I21]

Pirineo Pyrenees mountains [I18]

piruétano wild pear [II13]

pisacorto slow-footed [I23]

pisada step [I46]

pisado stepped on [I23]

pisar to trample [I14], to walk on [I28], to step onto [II1], to tread [II35]

pistolete pistol [II60]

pistos a, dar to nourish [II44]

pito whistle [II63]

pizmiento black [I38]

place, que me with pleasure [I6]

placer pleasure [I4], ease [I41]

placera market woman [II51]

plana page [reI]
plancha plaque [I52]
plano, de openly [II38]
planta foot [I42/43]
plantado set up [II58]
plañir to lament [I24]
plasmador framer [I46]
plata silver [I2], **de —** silvery [II35]
platica = practica happens [I33]
plática conversation [I5], discourse [I18]; practice [II49]
platicar to perform [II29]
plato plate [I52], dish [II47]
platonazo great big plate [II47]
platónico Platonic [I25]
plaza marketplace [I1], fortification [I39]; **salir a la** to come out [I33]
plazo term [I14], scheduled time [II55]
plebeyo plebeian [I50]
plega a Dios = plazca a Dios may it please God [I17]
plegar to deign [I2], **= pegar** to close [I12]
plegaria supplication [I20]
pleito lawsuit [I46], dispute [II56]
pliego folded sheet (book section) [tasa I], sheet [II19], bundle [II66]
plomo lead [I52], **ir con pie de —** to be circumspect [II32], **a —** straight down [I46]

pluguiera may it please [I16]
pluguiese may it please [II50]
pluma pen [prI], feather [I2]; **colchón de —** feather bed [II4]
plumaje feathered hat [I51], "feathers" [II61]
poblado town [I10]; full [II36]
pobre poor [I4]
pobrete unfortunate person [I22]
pobreza poverty [I37]
poco: por — almost [I2], **poco a — ** gradually [I21], **cuán de —** how unprepossessing [I29], **tener en —** hold in little esteem [I22]
podadera pruning knife [I1]
podar to prune [II53]
poder power [prI], authority [reI], **en — de** in the care of [I12]
poderío power [I8]
poderosísimo very powerful [II38]
poderoso mighty [I14], able [I27], powerful [I34]
podrida, olla stew [II47]
podrido rotted [I21], rotten [II51]
podrir to rot [II47]
poema poem [II16]
poesía poetry [I6]
poeta poet [prI]
polaco Polish [II62]
polaina legging [I28]
policía manners [II44]
polido = pulido nice looking

[I11], polished [II19]

polilla destroyer [I39]

político civilizado [II16]

polla young hen [II59]

pollina donkey filly [II10]

pollinesco referring to donkeys [I25]

pollino young donkey [II10]

pollo chicken [II59]

polo pole [II29]

poltrón lazy [prI]

polvareda cloud of dust [I18]

polvo dust [I5]

pólvora gun powder [I38]

polvorosa road [I21]

polvoroso dusty [I2]

pompa splendor [I12]

pomposidad pomposity [II52]

pomposo magnificent [I11], pompous [II52]

ponderar to consider [II2], to praise [II3]

poner to put down on paper [II3], to set table [II18], to establish [II47], **— fin** to end [I13], **—se a** to set about to [I27], to begin to [I12]; **—se en pie** to stand up [I28], **— en bando** to encourage [I28], **— a brazos** to fight [I34], **— en orden** to take care of [II50]

poniente, del on the east side [II63]

pontífico pontifical [II42]

ponzoña venom [I14]

popa poop [I39], **en —** from behind [II41]

por: — parte de by, **— cuanto** whereas, inasmuch as [reI], **— poco** almost [I2], **de su —** on his behalf [II10], **de la — de** from [II20]

porfía obstinacy [I14], insistence [I34]

porfiado fierce [I39]

porfiar to insist [I3], to importune [I14], to argue stubbornly [I44]

poro pore [II39]

porque so that [I2]

porqué reason [I35], **un buen —** a good amount [I13]

porquero swineherd [I2]

porrazo blow [I17]

porro blockhead [II5]

portador bearer [II50]

portal gate [I2]

portamanteo suitcase [II50]

portante quick pace, ambler [II40]

portar to behave [II56]

portazgo toll [I45]

porte postage [II51]

portería gatehouse [I36]

portero doorman [I14]

portillo gate [II53]

porvenir future [II25]

posada stay [I3], dwelling [I6], lodging [I17], inn [I42/43], place to stay [II25]

posaderas buttocks [I20]
posar to lodge [I11]
posas buttocks [II35]
poseedor possessor [II6]
poseer to keep [I23], to possess [I34]
posesión land [I21], possession [II7]
posesor possessor [I33]
posibilidad means [I40]
posibilitado allowed [I52]
posible, a mi as much as I could [II43]
poso rest [II19]
posta: por la — right away [I15], **a —** on purpose [I29], intentionally [II6], **corneta de la —** post horn [II47]
postema abscess [aprob. II]
postillón courier [II34]
postizo artificial [I11], wig [II21]
postrar to demolish [II38]
postre dessert [II47]
postrero last [II22]
postura position [I9]
potencia possibility [I15]
potestad power [II1]
poyo bench [I51]
pozo well [I3]
pradecillo little meadow [I20]
prado field [I6], meadow [I20]
pragmática decree [II51]
prazga may it please (rustic form of **placer**) [I10]
preámbulo preamble [I33]

precedencia priority [II64]
preceder to precede [I27]
precepto precept [I48]
preceto = **precepto** precept [I8]
preciado esteemed [II8]
preciar to value [I6], **—se de** to take pride in [I13]
precio value [I21], price [I41]
preciosísimo very precious [I5]
precioso precious [I46]
precipitarse to rush [I20]
precipitosamente hurriedly [I34]
preciso clear [I49]
predicador preacher [I18]
predicamento prestige [I42]
predicar to preach [prI]
preeminencia superiority[I38], privilege [I45]
prefación preface [prI]
pregón proclamation [I28]
pregonar to proclaim [I14]
pregunta question [I24]
preguntante question asker [I42/43]
preguntar to ask [I7]
premática *mod.* **pragmática** decree [reI]
premiar to reward [prI]
premio prize [I24], reward [I42/43]
prenda jewel [I6], article [I23], treasure [I33], security [I27], pledge [I40]; **—s** reward [I34], **buenas —s** worth [II16]
prender to arrest [I5], to take

[I33]

preñado pregnant, full [I40]

preñez pregnancy [II43]

preparado prepared [II20]

prerrogativa privilege [I37]

presa dam [I20], prize [I41], grip [I45], weight [pról II], booty [II60]

presea precious object [II60]

presencia presence [I27], appearance [II47]

presentado as a present [I1], advanced divinity student [I25]

presentar to present [II47], **—se** to appear [I1]

presente gift [I25], **—s** those who were present [I42]

preso prisoner [I15], arrested [II11]

prestado lending [II45]

prestar to lend [prI]

presteza haste [I7], nimbleness [I16]

presto soon [I3], quickly [I14], quick [I34], **de —** promptly [I22]

presumir to pride oneself [I16], to suppose [I41]

presunción vanity [I13], presumption [I51]

presuntuoso presumptuous [II74]

presuponer to presuppose [II26]

presupuesto goal [I7], being so

[I28], since [I29], purpose [II55]

presuroso hasty [II21], anxious [II62]

pretender to press suit [I11], to try [I33], to look for [I44], to want [aprob. II]

pretendiente suitor [I51]

pretensión character [I20], aim [I28]

pretérito past [I25]

pretina belt [I4], **dar con una —** to whip with a belt [I4]

prevaricador corruptor [II19]

prevención prevention [I28], preparatory statement [I33], precaution [II1]

prevenciones preparations [I2], provisions [I3], precautions [I48]

prevenido ready [I41], forewarned [II63]

prevenir to prevent [I21], to foresee [I37], **—se** to be prepared [I27], to prepare oneself [I28], **—se de** to arrange [II16]

previlegio *mod.* **privilegio** copyright, [reI]

previsto foreseen [II24]

prez trophy [I7], glory [I29]

priesa = prisa haste [I1], pregnant [II41], skirmish [II53], crush of people [II62]; **dar — a** to harass [II17]

prima hermana first cousin [I22]

primavera spring [II53]

primera order [I25]

primeramente firstly [I30]

primero first [I1]; — **que** before [I7]; —**s movimientos** first impulses [I30]

primo first [I11]; cousin [I21]

primor beauty [I23], delicacy [II47]

princesa princess [I1]

principal renowned [I2], upper class [I36], main [II9]

principalidad high estate [I25]

principalmente mainly [II23]; high [II32]

príncipe prince [dedI], important person [II2]

principio beginning [tasa I]

priora prioress [I35]

prioste steward [I21]

prisa, darse to hurry [I6]

prisión prison [I40], arrest [I45]

prisiones fetters [I22]

prístino original [II32]

privado favorite [I40]

privanza favor [I24]

privar to deprive [II10]

privilegio copyright [priv. I]

pro *arch.* benefit [I2], dignity [I25], **de** — worthy [II25]

proa prow of ship [I38]

probanza evidence [I22]

probar to attempt [I4], to test [I1], to prove [I13], to taste [I21], to try [I33]

proceder to issue [I2], to come from [II12]; behavior [I14]; — **en infinito** unending [II69]

proceloso tempestuous [II1]

procesión procession [I52]

procrear to procreate [II38]

procurador lawyer [I22]

procurar to try to [prI], to want to obtain [I28], to make sure [II71]

prodigalidad lavishness [II20]

prodigioso wonderful [pról. II], monstrous [II36]

pródigo lavish [I39], generous person [II17], extravagant [II67]

proeza feat [I3]

profanar to dishonor [I27]

profano secular [prI]

profecía prophecy [I30]

profesar to practice [I1], to participate [II63]

profesión profession [I2]

profesor one who professes [I37]

profeta prophet [II62]

profetizar to prophesy [II23]

profundamente deeply [I34]

profundidad depths [II8]

profundísimo very deep [II23]

profundo deep [I27], depths [II51]

progreso progression [I13]

prójimo fellow creature [I16]

prolijidad verbosity [II26]

prolijo long-winded [I51], long [II44]

prólogo prologue [prI]
prolongado prolonged [II48]
promesa promise [I1], vow [II67]
prometer to promise [I1], to allow [I44], to lead one to believe [II20]
prometido promised [I14]
prometimiento promise [I28]
promontorio cape [I41]
promovido promoted [I39]
prompto = **pronto** [I11]
pronosticado foretold [I46]
pronto ready [I3]
pronunciado pronounced [I4]
propias womenfolk [II42]
propincuo near [I15]
propio proper [I3], one's own [I14], messenger [ded. II], itself [II44]
proponer to propose [I6], to present [I12]
proporcionado proportioned [II42]
propósito aim [I2], subject matter [I2], intention [I24], purpose [I31]; a — properly [I48], fit for [I4], aptly [I5]; **de** — earnestly [I31], intentionally [I41]; **hacer al** — to apply [I33]
propriedad = **propiedad** propriety [I6], property [I21], appropriateness [I9], qualities [II62]
proprio = **propio** proper [I25], itself I41], one's own [I51]

propuesto proposed [I39]
prosa prose [I1]
prosapia ancestry [I13]
proseguir to continue [I2]
prosopopeya pomposity [II36]
próspero fair [I29], favorable [I39]
prosuponer to suppose [II49]
prosupuesto = **presupuesto** goal [I3], resolve [II12], object [II35]; — **que** since [I33], given [I37]
protestar to assure [I49], to warn [II17]
protoencantador protoenchanter [II41]
provecho profit [prI], benefit [I15], use [I17],
provechoso beneficial [reI], useful [II43]
proveedor provider [I18]
proveer to provide [I10], to decide a case [I22], —**se** to supply oneself [I7]
proveído supplied [I3], appointed [I42]
providencia providence [I25], foresight [II12]
provincia province [I7]
provocado provoked [I25]
prudencia circumspection [dedI], prudence [I22], judiciousness [I25]
prudente judicious (person) [prI]
prudentísimo very judicious [II2]
prueba proof [I10], attempt [I40],

a — y estése remand [II26]

pública voz common knowledge [II7]

publicador publisher [I46]

públicamente publicly [I35]

publicar to proclaim [I14], to make known [I28]

público public [I5]

pucheritos, con whimpering [II44]

puchero stew-pot [II20], hacer —s to sob [II74]

pudrir to rot [I17], —se to get angry [II43]

pueblo town [I1]

pueda may [II74]

puente bridge [I32], — levadiza drawbridge [I2]

puerco pig [I2]; foul [II43]

puerta gate [I2], — falsa back door [I2], a — cerrada wholly [II74]

puerto port [I30], tomar — to land [I15], — seguro safe port [II60]

pues then [I2], since [I1], — que although [prI]

puesto having put [I1], set [I8], equipped [I42/43], determined [I52]; position [I42], place [II20]; — que although [I2], even if [I27], — caso que although [I33]

pugnar (por) to struggle to [I4]

pulcela maiden *Ital.* [II44]

pulga flea [I30]

pulgares "fingers" [I22]

pulir to polish [I18], to pluck [II40]

pulla rude remark [II10]

púlpito pulpit [II3]

pulpo octopus [II19]

pulso pulse [II4], steady hand [II19]

punta extremity, tip [I7], promontory [I20], point [I21], de — en blanco from head to foot [II11], —s y collar smatterings [I22], —s y remates borders [I27], —s de randas lace [II52]

puntada, dar to persist [I33], to start [II28]; no dar — not to have the least idea [II62]

puntería aiming [II54]

puntiagudo sharp [pról. II]

puntillazo kick [II63]

puntillo small point [II58]

punto detail [I1], instant [I2], moment [I4], stitch [I30], point [I40], position [I41], bit [II31]; a — ready [I39], exactly [I46], al — immediately [I31], a un — at the same time [I27], instantly [I28]; en un — immediately [I1]; luego al — immediately [I3], — y término point [I8], en su — up to the mark [I14], at its greatest [I41], in perspective [I42], just right [II62]; ready

[I17], in the right place [I20], — **de reposo** a moment's rest [I16], **a — de** about to [I18], **de todo** — completely [I19], in perspective [I20], — **de** ready to [I20], **poner en su** — to appreciate [I37], **poner en su** — to come to a conclusion, **tomar —s** to darn [II2], **a cada** — constantly [II27], de — en punto **with each moment** [II68]

puntoso suspicious [II1]

puntual accurate [I9], conscientious [II64]

puntualidad exactness [prI], diligence [II23], **con toda —** scrupulously [I3]

puntualísimo very punctual [I16], very accurate [II50]

puntualmente exactly [I12]

puntuoso affected [II50]

punzamiento puncturing [II69]

punzar to puncture [II39], to sting [II68]

punzón awl [II48]

puñada punch [I16]

puñado handful [I39]

puñal dagger [I15]

puñalada stab [II33]

puñalero poniard maker [II23]

puño fist [I11], handful [I11], hilt of a sword [I14], punch [I44], cuff [II70]

pupilo orphan [I3]

purgar to purge [I6], to give an enema [II47]

purgatorio purgatory [I25]

puridad secret [II52]

purísimo very pure [I21]

puro pure [I41], **a —** by dint of [I33]

púrpura de Tiro Tyrian purple [I11]

pusilanimidad cowardliness [II41]

puta whore [I16]

putería lewd acts [II13]

puto bugger [II13]

puto sodomite [II29]

Q

que, no not to mention [I33]

qué how many [II62], **a qué** for what reason [II51]

quebrada narrow pass [I23]

quebradizo yellow [II23]

quebrado broken [I8]

quebrantado crushed [I39], pounded [I5]

quebrantamiento fracture [I15], bruises [I17]

quebrantar to break [II49]

quebrantar to break [II35]

quebranto grief [I14]

quebrar to break [I33]

quedada stay [I34]

quedar to become [I3], to be [I1], to remain [I4], to agree [I47], to submit [II14], to settle [II4], — **en pie** to stand firm [I34], **—se** to be put off [I7], to remain [I21], **— por** to remain, i.e. to do [35]

quedito very quietly [II48]

quedo quiet [I4], still [II14]

queja grumbling [I17], complaint [I23]

quejarse to complain [I4], to lament [I1]

quemar to burn [I5]

querella complaint [I14]

querellante complainant [II45]

querencia direction towards the stable [I4], haunt [I27], home [II13]

querer will [I20]; to accept [II14], **— bien** to love [I20]

querido lover [I16]

queso cheese [I10]

quicio hinge [I10]

quiebra fissure [I11], gap [I13], crack [II19]

quien the person who [I20], which [II22], anyone [II23]

quienquiera whoever [I3], nobody [II33]

quietarse to become quiet [I2], to rest [I52]

quieto peaceable [I15]

quietud tranquility [I3], repose [prI], stillness [I16], calm [I41]

quijada jawbone [I16], jaw [I29]

quilatar to test [I33]

quilate degree of perfection [I33], carat [I33]

quimera chimera [I14]

quimérico fanciful [I13]

quimerista troublemakers [II3]

quince días two weeks [I7]

quínola four of a kind in cards [II31]

quinta esencia quintessence [I29]

quinto fifth [I13], **tercio y —** greatly [II31]

quiriendo = **queriendo** wanting [II10]

quiso he agreed [I35]

quistión = **cuestión** quarrel [I29], dispute [I45]

quisto, mal hated [II10]

quitación salary in addition to board [II24]

quitado taken out [I7], taken off [II16]

quitar(se) to take away [I1], to take off [I35], to remove [I4], to relieve [I10], **—se** to go away [I8], **— el sueño** to wake up [I16], **— la vida** to kill [I41]

quitasol parasol [I4]

quito free [I35]

quizá perhaps [prI]

R

rabel rebec [I11]

rabia rage [I9]

rabiar to seethe with rage [I9], to

be furiously eager [II9]

rabioso furious [I51]

rabo tail [I21]

rabultado matted [I23]

racimo bunch (of grapes, dates) [II21]

ración portion [I2], income [II24]

rafigurar to recognize [II54]

raíces property [I12]

raído scraped [II55]

raigón root [II57]

raíz root [I44]

raja shred, slice [I6], **— de Florencia** a fine cloth [I6]

rajar to split [I52]

rajita little slice [II66]

ralea breed [I4], kind [II38]

rallar to scrape [I42/43]

ralo with gaps [II23]

rama branch [I25]

ramal rope [II36]

ramera prostitute [prI]

ramo branch [I8], bouquet [I14]

rana frog [II42]

rancho small room [I16], hut [II29], jail cell [I40]

rancioso old [I28]

rancor = rencor animosity [I9]

randado lace-trimmed [II47]

randas lace [II18], **puntas de —** lace [II52]

randera lacemaker [II70]

rapacería childish prank [II49]

rapador barber [II1]

rapamiento shaving [II40]

rapar(se) to shave [I21]

rapaza young girl [I12]

rapiña prey, **aves de —** birds of prey [II22]

rapista barber [II1]

raposa fox [I29]

raras veces infrequently [I3]

raro extravagant [I11], strange [I23], rare [I39]

rasa smooth [I18]

rascarse to scratch one another [II12], to scratch oneself [II22]

rasgado torn [I20], strumming [I51]

rasgar to tear [I25]

rasguño sketch [II32]

raso smooth [I18], satin [I27], **en campo —** in the open air [I19], **silla rasa** plain saddle [II10]

rastrear to drag [I18], to investigate [I23], to skim the ground [II40]

rastrillado combed [I28]

rastrillar to comb [I25]

rastrillo iron grating over gate [II71]

rastro trail [II14], slaughterhouse [II20]

rastrojos harvested field [I2]

rata prorated [I20], **— por cantidad** prorated [II28]

ratero trivial [I16]

rato period of time [I1], rat [I16]

raudal swift current [II29]

raya line [I34], border [II26], **a —**

within limits [I3], within bounds [I8], **echar** — to surpass [II47]

rayar en to approach [I39]

rayo ray [I7], lightning bolt [I18]

raza race [I28]

razón reason [I1], rational faculty [I1], word [prI], consideration [I2], justice [I4], argument [I38]; **ser** — to be right [I1], **estar a** — to be reasonable [II16], **por** — **de** because of [I14], **con** — reasonably [I27], **con buena** — reasonably [I19], **dar** — to explain [I35]

razonable reasonable [I7], proper [I41]

razonado, bien well-spoken [II32]

razonamiento speech [I11], conversation [II3]

razonar to talk [I25]

real Spanish silver coin worth 34 **maravedís** [I1]; spoils [I21]; royal [I21], — **Consejo** Royal Council [I32]

realzar to enhance [II4]

rebaño flock [I18]

rebenque whip [II63]

rebién very well [I23]

rebullir to come to life [II69]

rebuznar to bray [II25]

rebuzno bray [II8], braying [II25]

recado message [I20], profit [I37], provisions [I48], feed [II25],

mal — injury [I15], carelessness [I23]

recámara bedroom [I27]

recambio reciprocation [I27]

recapacitar to remind [II43]

recatado modest [I24]

recatarse to be cautious [I34]

recato modesty [I12], prudence [I12], reserve [I42]

recebía = **recibía** [I1]

recebían = **recibían** [I3]

recebido = **recibido** received [I3], accepted [I49]

recebir = **recibir**

recelarse to suspect [I24], to become suspicious [I24]

recelo fear [I35]

receloso fearful [II19]

receta recipe [I10], prescription [aprob. II]

recetado prescribed [I27]

rechinante to creak [II34]

reciamente strongly [II14]

recibir to accept [I4], to greet [I13]

recio strong [I1], hard to bear [I25], loud [I50], hard [II71]

recíproco reciprocal [I33]

recitante actor [II11]

recitar to recite [I25]

reclusión seclusion [II15]

recluso in seclusion [I6]

recobrar to recover [II35]

recoger(se) to gather (together) [I2], to take shelter [I2], to lock up [I33], to retire [42]

recogido received [I11], crouching [I16], reserved [I33], secluded [II46]

recogimiento privacy [I12], concentration [I11], seclusion [II1]

recompensa compensation [I11]

recompensar to recompense [I47]

reconciliado reconciled [I28]

reconciliarse to be reconciled [I40]

reconocer to recognize [I27]

recordación remembrance [I8]

recordar to wake up [II41]

recorrer to examine [I17]

Recorrido having run fingers over [strings of instrument] [II44]

recostado leaning [I42/43]

recostar to court [I3], —**se** to lean against [I50]

recreación recreation [I48]

recrear to gladden [I24], —**se** to enjoy [I47]

recto straight [I20], direct [I29]

rector principal, head [II1], headmaster [II47]

rectoría office of principal [ded. II]

rectórico eloquent [I48]

recua drove of mules, horses [I3]

recuesto slope [I47]

red net [I21]

redecilla harinet [II49]

redemir = redimir: — su vejación to relieve one's vexation [II35]

redención recovery [I2]

redoma flask [I10]

redonda, a la around [I11]

redondez roundness, face [of earth] [I19]

redondo round [I33]

redropelo, a against one's will [II12]

reducir to convert [prI], to come to [I23], to restore [I27], to persuade [I28], to bring [I30], to convince [II7]; —**se** to reconfirmed oneself [II65], to stay [II73]; — **a cuenta** to count [I38]

redundar to redound [I3]

refacción nourishment [I50]

referido mentioned [I3]

referir to relate [I3], —**se a** to refer to [tasa II]

refocilarse to have recreation [I15], to enjoy [II22]

reforzar to make loud [I16]

refrán saying, proverb [I7]

refrancico little proverb [II28]

refriega fray [I18]

refrigerio comfort [I37]

refugio refuge [I36]

regaladamente pleasantly [I27]

regaladísimo well entertained [II18]

regalado well-stocked [I8], pampered [I28], delicate [I42/43]

regalar to entertain [I11], to pamper [I28], to caress [I42/43]

regalo pleasure [prI], joy [I24], comfort [I37], luxury [II18]

regañar to argue [II70]

regatón hoarder [II51]

regazo lap [II45]

regenta president of the court of justice's wife [II60]

regente president of the court of justice [II60]

regidor alderman [II25]

regimiento municipal council [II45]

región = legión legion [I45]

regir to rule [I4], to control [II14], to direct [II63]

registro register book [I22]

regocijadamente joyfully [I8]

regocijado happy [II5]

regocijador merrymaker [II7]

regocijar to gladden [I33]

regocijo merriment [I19], joy [I45], —s festivities [I22]

regodeo jest [I22]

regoldar to belch [II43]

regostare to take a fancy to [II69]

regüeldo belch [II43]

rehacerse to rally [I19]

rehuir to refuse [I28]

rehusar to refuse [I26], to not accept [II18]

reina queen [I4]

reinar to reign [I47]

reino kingdom [reI]

reinocorporarse to reconcile oneself [II65]

reír to laugh [I3]

reiterar to reiterate [II18]

reja grate [I21], — **del corvo arado** plow [I11]

rejal stack of bricks laid criss-cross [II20]

rejo strength [I25]

relación report [reI], telling [I9], account [II7]

relatar to relate [II10]

relente lack of care [II53]

relieve relief [II58]

relieves leftovers [I20]

religión order [I39], religion [II8]

religioso friar [I8]

relinchar neighing [I18]; to neigh [II8]

relincho neigh [II4]

reliquia relic [I18], vestige [I41], holy relic [I33], —s remains [II26]

reloj clock [I33]

relucir to sparkle [II7]

relumbrar to shine [I21]

remachar to flatten [I52]

remanecer to reappear suddenly [I12]

remanso sluggishness [II17]

rematadamente utterly [I38]

rematado terminated [I1],

complete [II33]

rematar to finish [I19]

remate end [I40], **como —** on top of it all [I35], **puntas y —s** borders [I27]

remediar to remedy [prI], to help [I45], to put a stop to [II16]

remedio remedy [I5], medicine [I24], measures [I40]

remendado mended [II2], spotted [II10]

remendón clothes mender [I3]

rementir to lie [I45]

remero rower [I41]

remiendo patch [II44]

remirar to inspect [I24]

remisión pardon [I6], seclusion [I33], postponement [II67]

remiso remiss [II32]

remitir to submit [I50], to send [II21], **—se** to defer [I45]

remo oar [I39]

remojado marinated [I2]

remolino barrier of people [I52]

remondarse el pecho to clear one's throat [II46]

remontar to soar [II41]

remorder to cause remorse [II31]

remoto remote [I25]

remunerar to pay [I21]

renacuajo tadpole [I18]

rencilla quarrel [II25]

renco limping [II44]

rencuentro fight [I38], encounter [II12]

rendición recovery [I2]

rendido obsequious [I1], subdued [I18], surrendered [I4]

rendir to overcome [I1], to give back [I23], to deliver [I40], to subdue [I41], to yield [II25]; **—se** to surrender [I9]

rendirse to surrender [I34]

renegado renegade [I40]

renegar to change religions [I40], to complain [I51], to disown [II13]

renglón written line [prI]

renglones, entre as afterthoughts [I21]

reniego execration [I15]

renombre epithet [I32], renown [I48]

renovar to reiterate [I29], to rebuild [I52], to remind [II1], to renovate [II1], to revive [II1], to renew [II3]

renquear to limp [II30]

renta income, **— rentada** fixed income [I26]

renunciar to give up [I10]

reñido hard-fought [I16], bitter [I21]

reñir to scold [I28], to argue [I32], to fight [II14]

repacejo fringe [II49]

reparar to consider [prI], to stop [I30], to ward off [II59], **— de** to supply with provisions [I29], **— en** to wait for [I27], to take notice [I28], —se to protect oneself [I3]

repartible, no what cannot be distributed [II60]

repartición distribution [II60]

repartido distributed [I24]

repartir to divide [I40], to distribute [I41]

repasar to go back over [II51]

repelón rapid attack on horseback [II55]

repente, de sudden [II24]

repentino unexpected [I27], sudden [I34]

repicar to ring [II19],

réplica objection [I4], appeal [I6]

replicar to respond [prI], to argue [I7], to say [I8], to dispute [I12], to contradict [I13], to say [II41]

reportar(se) to refrain [I20]

reposadamente calmly [II32]

reposado quiet [I2], calm [II8]

reposar to rest [I22]

reposo tranquility [I3], repose [I13], rest [I41]

repostería luggage [II34], larder [II59]

repostero sumpter cloth [II73]

reprehender to reprimand [I36], to reprehend [II16]

reprehendido = reprendido blamed [I14]

reprehensión reprimand [I4], reprehension [aprob. I]

reprehensor reprehensor [aprob. II]

representación play [II19]

representado put on, as a play [ded. II]

representante actor [I48]

representar to make appear [I2], to occur [I9], to dramatize [I34], to represent [I40], to put on a play, to act [I48], —se to picture [I27]

reprimir to control [I30]

reprochar to reject [I2], to reproach [I17]

reproche rebuke [I11]

reprueba more proof [II26]

reptar to challenge [II52]

república republic [I38]

repuesto provisions [I19], cabinet [I34]

repugnar to oppose [I27]

repulgado affected [II40], with border [II48]

reputado renowned [II14]

requebrar to court [I12]

requerido courted [I33]

requerir to require [I18], to put on [I29] to persuade [II17], to investigate [I34] — de amores to court [I28]

requesones cottage cheese [II17]

requestar to court [I3]

requiebro love story [I1], flattery [I16], flirtatious remark [II21]

requirimiento demand [II17]

requirir = requerir to require [I49]

requisito requirement [II16]

res head of cattle [I18]

resbalar to slip off [I42/43]

resbaloso slippery [I20]

rescatado ransomed one [I40]

rescatarse to ransom oneself [I40]

rescate ransom [I39]

rescebido = recibido [I33]

rescibió = recibió [I4]

resentirse to recover senses [I15], to feel the effects [I42/43], to take offense [II1]

reservado retained [I14]

resfriar to cool [I24], **—se** to catch cold [II71]

residencia, en when I leave office [II47]

residir to reside [tasa II]

resistir to resist [I33]

resolución resolve [I20], **en —** in short [prI]

resoluto resolved [I33]

resolverse to resolve [I35]

resonar to resound [I12]

respecto regard [prI]

respeto observance [I11], respect [I3], account [I35]

respirar to breathe [I35]

resplandecer to shine [I41]

resplandeciente shining [II10], bright [II25]

resplandor brightness [I16], flash [I38]

responder to answer [I7], to respond [I27], to correspond [I44]

respondiente answerer [II62]

respondón responding [II62]

respuesta answer [I4]

resquebrajo crack (error for **requiebro**) [II10]

resquicio gap [I11], crack [pról II]

restar to remain [I3]

restituido restored [I29]

restituir to restore [I29]

resucitador reviver [II25]

resucitar to come back to life [I1], to revive [I7]

resuelto resolved [I26]

resultar to turn out [I22]

retablo portable theater [II25], altarpiece [II58]

retama broom branch [I25]

retar to challenge [I44]

retazos bits and pieces [II47]

retintín sound [II40]

retirada withdrawal [II67]

retirado withdrawn [II9]

retirar to take away [I3], **—se** to withdraw [I16], to retire [II70]

retor = rector

retórica rhetoric [prI]

retórico rhetorician [prI]

retorno return [I16], **de —** rental [II40]

retozar to frolic [II38], **— la risa en el cuerpo** to repress laughter [II32]

retraer to take refuge [I10]

retratado etched [I42/43]

retratarse de to retract [II24]

retrato portrait [I4], appearance [II16]

retrete secret room [II62]

retular = rotular to inscribe [II73]

rétulo = rótulo sign [I9]

retumbar to resound [II26]

reuma abscess [I18]

revalidar to revive [I10], to retaliate [I26]

reventar to burst [I3]

reverencia, hacer to bow [II10]

reverenciar to revere [I45]

reverendísimo very reverent [II48]

reverendo reverent [I29]

revés backhand slash [I1], change [I24], diagonal slash, left to right [II19], **al —** the other way around [I22], **por el — from the back** [II62]

revivir to revive [I52]

revocar to revoke [II44]

revolcar to knock down [II7]

revoltillo mess [II43]

revolver to turn [I18], to return [II19], **—se** to turn around [I19]

revuelta deviation [prI]

revuelto convoluted [I6], encumbered [I19], wrapped [I35]

rey king [I7]

rezar to pray [I3], to read [I45]

ribera shore [I18], bank (of river) [II28]

ribete trimming [I27], hem [II38]

ricamente richly [I21]

rico rich [I4]

ridículo laughable [II3]

rienda rein [I2]; **a — suelta** rashly [I3], **tener las —s** to rein in [II16]

riendo laughing [I4]

riesgo risk [I36], **estar al —** to withstand [I1]

rieto = reto I challenge [I44]

rigor severity [dedI], **por todo —** to the extremes [II56]

riguridad harshness [II58]

rigurosamente severely [I15]

riguroso critical [I25], rigorous [I2], severe [I7]

rijoso lustful [I15]

rimero heap [I6]

rincón corner [I1], nook [I23]

riña quarrel [pról. II]

riñón kidney [II18]

río river [prI]

ripio rubble [II4]

riqueza wealth [I12], richness [II58], **—s** riches [I41]

risa laughter [prI], **de —** laughable [I52]

risco stone [I11], cliff [I14]

ristre lance rest [I8]

risueño smiling person [prI]; smiling [I20], laughable [I52]

robado kidnaped [I21], robbed [I26]

robador robber [I8]

robar to rob [I1], to kidnap [I21]

roble oak tree [I8]

robo robbery [I23]

robusto robust [I11]

roca rock [I34]

rociar to sprinkle [I6]

rocín nag [I1]

rocino *arch.* **rocín** [I2]

rocío moisture [I52], dew [I49]

rodado dappled [I21]

rodaja wheel [II19]

rodar to roll [I4]

rodeado surrounded [I33]

rodear to move [I8], to go all the way around [I17], to surround [I1], to arrange [I26], to roam [II5], to turn [II41]

rodela round shield [I7]

rodeo circumlocution [I11], roundabout way [I42]

rodilla knee [I1], **de** — on one's knees [I29], — **de aparadores** dishrag [II32]

roer to gnaw [I34], — **los zancajos** to backbite [II36]

rogación entreaty [II22]

rogar to implore [I2], to beg [I22], to pray [I10], to court [I13], to ask [I50]; **de** — urging [I11]

rogativa prayers for rain [I52]

roído gnawed [I26]

rollizo plump [I20]

roma, nariz flat nose [I16]

romadizado with a cold [I31]

romance ballad [I2], Spanish [I40]

romancista writer in Spanish [II16]

romano Roman [I13], striped [II20], **a lo** — in a toga [II69]

rombo rhombus [II35]

romero rosemary [I11], pilgrim [II41]

romper to break [prI], to tear up [II16]; **al** — **del alba** at daybreak [I34]

rompido (*mod.* **roto**) broken [I4]

roncar to snore [II14]

ronco hoarse [I14]

ronda patrol [II49]

rondar make the rounds [II49]

rondón, de rashly [II32], headlong [II60]

ronquillo a bit hoarse [II46]

ropa clothing [I19], merchandise [II71], **hacer a toda** — to rob everything [I41]

ropilla doublet [I22]

ropón gown [I21]

rosa rose [I13]

rosado crimson [I2]

rosario rosary [I26]

rosca coil [II23]

rostro face [I1], **dar** — to face [I19], **hacer mal** — **a** to be cool toward [I35], **hacer** — to face [II32]

roto broken [I8], ragged [I13],

torn [I23]

rotura hole [I16]

rozagante flowing [II35]

roznar to bray [II29]

rúa, de in street clothes [II62]

rubí ruby [I50]

rubicundo blond [I2]

rubio golden [I18], blond [II39], blondness [II58]

rubión reddish wheat [I31]

rubricado initialed [reI]

rucio silver grey [I21]

rueca distaff [II65]

rueda wheel [I34], spread of a peacock's tail [I42], **en la —** present [I45], **— de molino** millstone [II6]

ruego supplication [I17], request [I41]

rufián ruffian [I34]

rugido roar [II5]

rugir roar [I14]

ruibarbo rhubarb [I6]

ruido noise [prI], clamor [I7], dispute [I8]

ruin vile [I4], frail [II35]

ruina fall [I9], disaster [I17], perdition [I30], **—s** ruins [I20]

rumiar to meditate on [II31]

rumor noise [I20], murmuring [II9]

rumpante rampant [I46]

rus nonsense word euphemism for **Dios** [II25]

rusticidad rusticity [II67]

rústico coarse [I27], peasant [I50]

rutilante shining [II35]

S

sábado Saturday [II25]

sábana sheet [I16]

sabandija vermin [II33]

saber to taste [I11]; **es de —** it should be made known [II17]

sabido known [I5], knowing [I11]

sabidor knower *arch.* [I15], confidante [I13]

sabiduría knowledge [I27], ingenuity [I31]

sabiendas, a knowingly [I47]

sabio wise person [I23]; **sabio,-a** sage [I2]

saboga shad [II29]

sabor pleasure [I15], taste [II13], **—es** likes [I23]

saborear to savor [II54]

saboyana skirt [I52]

sabrosamente deliciously [I34]

sabrosísimo very delicious [I51]

sabroso pleasant [I8], delicious [I11]

sacabuche primitive trombone [II27]

sacapotras quack [I24]

sacar to extract [I1], to take out [I1], to receive [II8], to stick out [II17], to gather [II37]; **— a luz** to publish [dedI], **— en limpio** to conclude [I18], **—le de**

sentido to drive one mad
[II28], — **a plaza** to show [II62]
sacerdote priest [I12]
saco bag [I20]
sacra escritura Bible [I49]
sacrificio sacrifice [I27]
sacrilegio sacrilege [I19]
sacristán sexton [I25]
sacristanía office of sexton [I26]
sacro holy [II8]
sacudiendo flapping [I22],
shaking [I28]
sacudir to beat [II11], to shake
[II14]
saeta arrow [I23]
sagacidad discernment [I21],
shrewdness [I25]
sagaz keen-witted [I34]
sagitario wise man [II54]
sagrada sacred [I19]
sahumado perfumed; with
interest [I4]
sahumerio interest [I4]
sal salt [I7]
sala parlor [I27], hall [I27]
salamanquesa salamander [II45]
salar to salt [I9]
salario salary [I18]
salida sally [I2]
salir to look on to [II62], to
promise [II63], —**le al camino**
to anticipate [II16]
saliva saliva [II13]
salmanticense Salmantine [II7]
salmantino person from

Salamanca [I6]
salpicón hash [I1]
salsa gravy [I19]
saltado protruding [II1]
saltaembarca cape [II49]
saltar(se) to bound [I22], to jump
[I39], to jump up [II10], to go
ashore [II1], to leap [II19], to
come out [II47]
salteador highwayman [I29]
saltear to snatch [I9], to take by
surprise [I15], to rob [II49]
salterio psaltery [II19]
salto jump [I21], leaps [II11], **a —**
by hops [I20]
salud health [prI], welfare [I15],
salvation [II6]
saludable sound [II11]
saludado greeted [I2]
saludar to greet [I8]
salutación salutation [I37
salutífero curative[I17]
salva oath [I48]; **hacer la —** to
have the first bite [II59], **a
mano —** easily [II73]
salvaje wild-man [I31]
salvamano, a without risk [II14]
salvar to avoid [II48], —**se** to
escape [I39], to save oneself
[II26]
salve the Salve Regina [I17]
salvo excepting [I6], sound [I20],
safety [I24], **a su —** without
injury, safely [I25]
salvoconduto permission [I25],

pass [II60]

sambenito penitent's shirt [II6]

sanado cured [I6]

sanar(se) to get better [I11], to cure [II18]

sandez folly [I2]

sandio foolish [I16]

sangrar to drain [I18], —**se** to be bled [I21]

sangre blood [I4]

sangría bloodletting [I4]

sangriento bloody [I52]

sanguíneo sanguine [II35]

sanguinolento bloody [I52]

sanidad health [I4], recovery [I1]

sano sound [I29], healed [I3], hale [I4], sound [I16], —**s de Castilla** "good people" [I2]

santa; non — unholy [I22], — **escritura** Holy Bible

santidad holiness [II44]

santiguada sign of the cross [I5]

santiguar to give the sign of the cross [I15], —**se** to cross oneself [II14]

santísimo very holy [I17]

santo saint [prI]; holy [I6], virtuous [II43]

santuario shrine [II54]

saña fury [I44]

sapo toad [II33]

sarao dancing party [II62]

sardesco small donkey [II27]

sardina arenque herring [I18]

sardo Sardinian [I6]

sarga painted fabric [II71]

sarna itch [I12]

sarta string of beads [I30]

sartén frying pan [II20]

sastre tailor [I45]

satanás satan [I5]

sátira satire [II1]

satírico satirical [II20]

sátiro satyr [I25]

satisfacer to settle [I2], to repay [I8], to atone [I14], to satisfy [I19], —**se** to satisfy oneself [I14]

satisfación = **satisfacción** [I4], confidence [I33], apology [II23], payment [II74]

satisfecho satisfied [I1], complete [I30]

sauce willow [II14]

saya skirt [I27], petticiat [II58]

sayagués rustic Leonese dialect [II19]

sayo tunic[I1], slip [I24]

sazón time [I20], opportunity [I40], **antes de toda** — prematurely [I2], **en** — **de** ready [I11],

sazonado ripe [I11], seasoned [II47]

scita = **escita** Scythian [II68]

secarle a uno to dry up [I1]

secarse to wilt [II53]

secas, a simply [I1],

seco dry [prI], dead [I8]; **en** — stranded [II8]

secretamente secretly [I34]

secretario guardian of a secret [I34]

secreto secret [I7], private [I13], anonymous [I15], **en su —** secretly [II51]

secta sect [I6], religion [I33]

secuaz underling [I45], follower [II21]

secutoria title [I45]

seda silk [I4], thread [I2]

sedero silk merchant [I9]

sediento thirsty [I13]

segador harvester [I32]

segar to cut [II39]

seglar secular [I6]

seguidamente straight [I20]

seguidillas light-hearted songs [II38]

seguido straight [I18]

seguidor follower [I46]

seguir to pursue [II53]

según according to [I1]

segundar to do a second time [I3], to repeat [I7]

segundo second [I6]

seguramente surely [dedI], safely [I41]

segurar to be sure [II2]

seguridad security [I17], safety [II41]

seguro certain [I7], safe [I23], unsuspicious [I27]; assurance [I24], **a buen —** it is certain [I13]

sellar to smack [II69]

sello seal [I48]

selva forest [I52], jungle [II17]

semblante face [I37], mien [II26]

sembradura sowing [I1]

sembrar to sow [I12]

semeja = semejanza resemblance [I12]

semejante like [prI], similar [I2], such [I2]

semejar to seem [I52]

semidoncella half-maiden [I42/43]

semínima musical quarter note [II40]

senado audience [II25]

sencilla simple [prI]; coin of little value [I2]

sencillez simplicity [II13]

sencillo coin of little value [I20]

senda path [I13]

sendero path [I52]

sendos one each [II41]

seno bosom [II11], bottom [II45]

sentado seated [II49]

sentencia maxim [prI], sentence [I7], opinion [I45], judgment [II66]

sentenciado, lo sentence pronounced against [II1]

sentenciar to pass judgment [II32]

sentible = sensible lamentable [I14]

sentido meaning [I1], sense [I14];

heard [I42/43]; heartfelt [I42/43]; **sin** — senseless [I8], heard [I20], unconscious [I41]

sentimiento pain [I5], feeling [I21]

sentir to hear [I16], to feel [I18], sympathize with [I28], to be aware [II11]; —**se** to resent [I19]

seña indication [II16], sign [II17], —**s** description(s) [II41], **por** —**s** by signs [II25]

señal mark [I1], sound [I2], sign [I15], indication [I25], token [I8]

señaladísimo very great [II30]

señalado designated [I40], determined [I13], named [I20], outstanding [I3], with bodily defect [II48]

señalando pointing [I22]

señalar to point out [I20], to fix (a date, etc.) [II52], to signal [II63]

señas bearings [I25], description [I27], **de** — by signs [I24], **por** — by signs [I40], **por más** — seemingly [I31], as further proof [I23]

señero alone [I11]

señor lord [I39], gentleman [tasa I], master [I1]; **Señor** Lord [I12]; **a lo** — in a lordly way [II62]

señora mistress [I1], lady [I1]

señorazo bigshot [II8]

señorear to govern [I13]

señoría ladyship [I2], lordship [II3]

señoril lordly [I46]

señorío dominion [I15], dignity [II5]

señorito little man [II10]

señuelo lure [I11]

sepultado buried [prI]

sepultar to cave in [I18], to bury [II8], to be shrouded [II53], —**se** to bury oneself [II22]

sepultura grave [I13]

sequedad dryness [I6], abruptness [I33]

ser being [I37]

serenar to clear up [I18]

serenidad serenity [prI]

sereno night air [I12]; serene [II35]

serga exploit [I6]

sermón sermon [I18]

sermoncico little sermon [prI]

serpiente snake [I14]

serrallo harem [II63]

serrezuela little mountain range [I23]

servicio service [prI], table setting [II47]

servido pleased [I3], **ser** — to please [reI]

servidumbre service [II13]

servil groveling [II32]

servir to serve [I2], to wait on

[I2], to repay [I24], — **de** to serve as [I2]; —**se** to be pleased [I40]; —**se de** to use [I41]

sesgo still [II21]

seso(s) brain [I2], wits [I23], **en — ** seriously [I50]

sestear to nap [I15]

sesto = sexto sixth [I21]

setenas sevenfold interest [I4]

severo harsh [aprob. II]

sí certainly [I40]; **por —** in itself, **entre —** to himself, etc. [I5]

Sicilia Sicily [II1]

siega harvest [I18]

siempre still [II9]

sien temple of head [I38]

sierpe serpent [I7]

sierra mountains [I12]

siesta afternoon nap (time) [I15]

siglo age [I1], epoch [I2], century [I13], life [I35], —**s** times [I39]

significar to represent [I4], to make known [I42/43], to indicate [I48]

significativo expressive [I1], meaningful [prI]

siguiente following [I18], **desde otro día —** on the next day [I33]

siguimiento pursuit [II26]

silbando whistling [II63]

silbato whistle [I2]

silbo whistle [I23], hiss [I14]

silencio silence [I13]

silguero = jilguero goldfinch

[II37]

silla saddle [I10], chair [I50], litter [II48], — **de manos** litter [II64]

sillón sidesaddle [I36]

silo silo [I46]

silvestre wild [I25]

silvoso wild [I18]

sima pit [I15]

simiente seed [I8]

similitud resemblance [I30]

simpar = sin par peerless [I4]

simple foolish, plain, simple person [prI], simple [I1], —**s** ingredients [I17]; simpleton [I22]

simpleza simplicity [II8]

simplicidad simplicity [I6]

simulacro image [I34]

sin par peerless [I4]

sinabafa fine fabric [I15]

sincero sincere [II1]

singular extraordinary [I1]

siniestro depravity [I15]; left [I23], catastrophic [II60]

sinificativo meaningful [II43]

sino except [I1], but [I8]

sinrazón injustice [I1]

sinsabor pain [I7], displeasure [I15], —**es** dislikes [I23]

siquiera at least [I16], even [I42/43], even for [I34], just [I6], although [pról. II], it makes no difference [II26]; — **no** not even [I34],

sirgo twisted silk [I11]
sirviente servant [II23]
sitio site [I20], location [II72]
so pena de under penalty of [I4]
sobajado manhandled [I26]
soberano sovereign [I25]
soberbia arrogance [I8], pride [II8]
soberbio arrogant [I1], splendid [II10]; arrogant person [I17]
sobornar to bribe [I28]
sobra excess [prI], leftovers [I37]
sobrado in excess [II13]
sobrar to be more than enough [I9], to be left over [II4]
sobre on [I41]
sobrecarga overload [II71]
sobredicho aforementioned [I1]
sobreescrito = sobrescrito address [II36]
sobrehumano superhuman [I13]
sobrellevar to help to bear [II51]
sobremanera beyond measure [I18]
sobremodo excessively [II23]
sobrenatural supernatural [I48]
sobrenombre (last) name [I1]
sobrepelliz surplice [I19]
sobrepujar to exceed [I23]
sobrerropa de levantar robe [II53]
sobresaltado startling [I33], terrified [I34], terrifying [II60]
sobresaltar to terrify [I16], to assail [I20], —se to be startled [I27], to jump on the inside [I42/43]
sobresalto fright [I8], fear [I34], distress [I42/43]
sobrescrito envelope [I27]
sobrevenir to follow [I20], to occur [I23], to befall [II48]
sobrina niece [I1]
sobrino nephew [II24]
socaliña cunning [II38]
socaliñado tricked [II40]
socapa, a surreptitiously [I46]
socarrón jokester [I3]
socarronería cunning [II43]
socorredor helper [II26]
socorrer to succor, aid [I3], to help [I35]
socorro help [I41]
soez vile [I3], coarse [I25]
soficiente = suficiente sufficient [II45]
sofistería deceitful nonsense [II51]
sofístico fallacious [I25]
soga rope [I14]
soguilla cord [II41]
sol sun [I2]
solapa, de on the sly [II33]
solapar to hide [II23]
solar ancestral mansion [I21]
solas: a — alone [I21], **a sus** — = **a solas** [I33]
solaz enjoyment [I11]
solazar to take one's ease [I2], —**se** to have pleasure [I19]

soldada wages [I4]

soldadesca soldiering [I39], pertaining to a soldier [I51]

soldado soldier [I1]

soldar to mend [I33], to solder [II19]

soledad privacy [I11], desert I13], solitude [I20], lonely place [I25]

solene = solemne solemn [I25], notorious [II7]

solenizado = solemnizado extolled [I23]

solenizar = solemnizar to commemorate [I41], to celebrate [I19]

soler to be accustomed [dedI], "used to" [I18]

solicitado wooed [I33], entreated [I12]

solicitar to make overtures [I7], to woo [I51]

solícito diligent [I11], insistent [I33], ready [I51]

solicitud importunity [I11], diligence [I28], persistence [I28]

soliloquio soliloquy [II10]

solitario solitary [I25]

sólito accustomed [II18]

sollozo sob [I27]

solo alone [I1], only [II23]

soltar to release [I4], to throw down [I3], to fire artillery [I41], —**se** to release oneself [I36]

soltero bachelor [I33]

soltura release [I22], run (in stocking) [II44]

sombra shadow [dedI], shade [I50]

sombras y lejos appearance [I17]

sombrero hat [I21]

sombrío sombre [I20]

sombroso shady [II12]

son = sonido sound [I4], music [II20]

sonado resounding [I1]

sonaja small hand drum [II19]

sonante sounding

sonar to sound [I2], to resound [I45]

sonda: con la — en la mano prudent [II32]

soneto sonnet, 14-line poem [I23]

sonoro clear [prI], sonorous [I1]

sonreírse to smile [I35]

sonsacar to entice away [II2]

soñado imagined [I1], dreamed [II25]

soñar to dream [I35]

soñoliento drowsy [I42/43]

sopa de arroyo stones [II11]

soplar to blow [I41]

sorber to soak up [II8]

sordo deaf person [I6]; quiet [I20]

sortija ring [I27]

sosegadamente calmly [II14]

sosegado calm [I5], still [I50]

sosegar to be comfortable [I18], to calm [I20], to calm down

[I20]; —se to become calm [II27]

sosiego tranquility [prI], calmness [I19]

soslayo, a obliquely [I7]

sospecha suspicion [I14]

sospechoso suspect [I33], suspicious [I48]

sospirar = suspirar to sigh [I12], to break wind [I8]

sospiro = suspiro [I17], fart [II8]

sostener to hold up [I20], —se to support oneself [I25]

sotaermitaño female sub-hermit [II24]

sota jack (playing card) [II25]

sotana cassock [I6]

sotiliza see sutileza

sotilmente slightly [I35]

suave gentle [prI], mixed together [II19]

suavemente quietly [II42]

suavidad mellowness [I6]

suavísimamente very gently [II44]

subir to mount [I2], to rise [I40], to help up [II10], to increase [II38]

súbito sudden [II29]

subjeto = sujeto [I14], —s matters [II2]

sublimado exalted [I46]

sublimidad loftiness [II41]

subsistir to live [I27]

suceder to happen [I7], to follow

in order [I16]

sucesivamente one after the other [I28]

suceso event [I5], success [I8], fortune [I12], outcome [I27], incident [II4]

sucintamente briefly [I16]

sucinto concise [I42]

sucio dirty [II25]

sudado sweaty [I31]

sudar to sweat [I5], — el hopo to sweat it out [I10]

sudor sweat [I4]

suegro father-in-law [II10], —s parents-in-law [I47]

suela sole of shoe [I26]

suelo ground [I3], floor [I16], earth [II43]

sueltas, echar to put fetters [I15]

suelto free [I12], loose [I22], agile [II20]

sueño sleep [I8], dream [I29], quitar el — to wake up, pesado — deep sleep [II42], — suelto sound sleep [II68]

suero whey [II17]

suerte kind [= type] [dedI], luck [I1], way [I17], fortune [I20], manner [I24], point [II49]; de — que so that [prI], state [I2], caberle la — to fall to one's lot [I4], de tal — in such a way [I17]; echar —s to draw lots [I12], desa — in that case

suficiencia capacity [II36]

sufragio services for the redemption of souls from purgatory [II55]

sufridor endurer [I50]

sufridor patient [I22]

sufrimiento patience [I25]

sufrir to endure [I4], to withstand [I16], to put up with [I17], to allow [II43]

sujeción weight [II53]

sujetarse to submit [I14]

sujeto object [I14], political subject [I41], subject [II42], opportunity [I47]; subjected [I2], humble person [II18]

sumar to amount to [tasa II]

sumergir to submerge [II23]

sumir to plunge [II14]

sumisión submission [II10]

sumiso low [II62]

sumo great [I39]

sumptuoso sumptuous [II34]

suntuoso sumptuous [I42/43]

supeditar to subdue [II18]

superchería outrage [II26], foul play [II28], fraud [II52]

superstición talisman [II52]

supino on one's back [II69]

suplemento supplement [II22]

suplicación request [I41]

suplicar to request [reI], to beg [prI], to entreat [I4]

suplicio punishment [I29]

suplir to supply [I1], to make up for [I1]

surco furrow [II35]

suso: de — above [reI]

susodicho aforesaid [priv. II]

suspender to stop [prI], to amaze [I42], to postpone [I51], to prop up [II4]

suspensión hesitation [prI], suspense [I33]

suspenso hesitant [prI], amazed [I9], in suspense [I22], bewildered [I51]

suspirar to sigh [I29]

suspiro sigh [I5]

sustancia substance [I10]

sustancial substantial [I16]

sustentar to sustain [I11], to feed [I15], to support [I39], to carry [I41],to hold up [I52]; **—se** to sustain oneself [I8], to be supported [I33]

sustento food [I10], sustenance [I31], support [II10]

susto fright [II11]

susurro rustling [I20], whisper [II33]

sutil slender [I3], subtle [II5]: thinness [I16]

sutileza light-fingeredness [I3], deftly [I10], sly [I23], subtlety [II8]

suyo, de by nature [I20]

T

tabaque, en in a basket [II43]
taberna tavern [pról. II]
tabí silk fabric [II58]
tabique partition [II59]
tabla panel [I2], table [I21], plank [I30], side [II10], **—s** backgammon [II26]; — **Redonda** Round Table [I17], **tabla rasa** *tabula rasa* empty slate [II46]
tablita little tablet [I25]
tacaño stingy [I52]
tacha blemish [I1], **poner —** to find a fault [II21]
tachar to charge [I23]
tácito quiet [I16], tacit [II25]

tacto touching [I16], sense of touch [II23]
tafetán fine silk [I27]
tagarina thistle [II13]
tahelí strap [I37]
tajadas, hacer to cut to pieces [II6]
tajadica little slice [II47]
tajado chiseled [I25]
tajadora trenchant [II46]
tajante sharp [II6]
tajar to cut [I30]
tajo slash [II26]
tal such a [prI], such a one [II1], in such a state [I31]; — **vez** perhaps [I7], some time [I11],

when [II23], sometimes [II45]; — **han parado** in such a state [I5]
taladrar [II33]
tálamo nuptial bed [I46]
talante mien [I2], state [II64]; **mal** — anger [I2]
talegazo blow with a sack [II14]
talego sack [I19], pockets [I26]
talle figure [I2], stature [I9], **buen** — good size [I4]; **a su —** in any way you want [I1], **en —** **de** ready to [II11]
tamaño so great [I3], so small [I4], as big as [I35]
también also [I3], **también = tan bien** [I1]
tamboril small drum [II20]
tamborín small one-handed snare drum [II67]
tamborino small drum [II19]
tanda batch [II40]
tangerino of Tangier [I40]
tantear to examine [I42], to measure [II37]
tanteo rough estimate [II60]
tantico a bit [prI]
tanto in fact [I35], an amount [I50]; **en —** meanwhile [I6], while [I25]; **en — que** until [I21], while [I41], as long as [I40]; **con — que** provided that [reI], **— cuanto** a little bit [I15], **en — que** while [I24]; **algún —** quite some time [I27], **— que**

enough so that [II44]

tantos so many [I39]

tañedor player [II20]

tañer to play [I6]

tapaboca hit on the mouth [II19]

tapar(se) to cover [I42/43]

tapiar to wall up [I7]

tapete rug [II63]

tapiz tapestry [I27]

tarazar to bite [I21]

tardanza delay [I13]

tardar(se) to delay [I2]

tardío slow [I46]

tardo slow [I47]

tártago anguish [II11]

tartamudo stammering [I46]

tartesio person from Andalucía [II12]

tasa price [tasa I], measure [I13], limit [II35]

tasajo piece of dried meat [I11]

tasar to fix a price [tasa I], to appraise [II4]

taza cup [I52]

teatro theater [I25], platform [II21]

techado, debajo de indoors [I12]

techo ceiling [I17]

tejado roof [I7]

tejedor weaver [II49]

tejer to weave [I6]

tejido woven [II31]

tejo yew [I13]

tela cloth [I6], web [I47], **las —s del corazón** heartstrings [I15],

pasar la — to enter the contests [I17]

telilla light wool material [I29]

tema mania [pról. II]

temblador trembling [II39]

temblar to tremble [I27]

temblor teeming [I42/43]

temer to fear [I2]

temerario reckless [II4], **juicio —** rash conclusion [I33]

temeridad recklessness [I49]

temeroso fearful [I8], terrified [I9], feared [I14], timid [I33]; terrified person [II68]

temido feared [I18]

temor fear [prI]

tempestad storm [I4]

templado warm [I50], mild [II23], temperate [II43]

templanza moderation [II62]

templar to tune an instrument [I11], to appease [I46], to blend [aprob. II], to turn [I41], to temper [I53], **—se** to moderate [I28]

temple temper [I25]

templo church [I33], temple [I18]

temprano early [I16]

ten moreover [II35], article of legal document [II74]

tenazas pincers [II45]

tender to spread out [I11], to extend [I16], **—se** to stretch out [I16]

tendera market seller [II51]

tendido spread out [I2], stretched out [I4], straight [I28], lying down [II58], **a pierna tendida** stretched out [II9]

tendilla open-air stand [I3]

tener to hold [I2], to contain [I2], to accept [II17], to come from [I24]; — **en poco** to care little [II16], — **por** to think [II2]; —**se** to stop [I4], — **fuerzas** to be strong enough [prI]; — **por** to consider [prI], — **por bien** to concur [reI], —**se** to stop [I5], — **ojo** to have regard [I12], — **cuenta con** to restrain [I28]

tenería tannery [II19]

tenido held [I40], thought[I39]

tenor tenor [I45], sort [II10], manner [II51], **por el propio —** in the same way [II62]

tentación temptation [I48]

tentar to grope [I7], to feel [I16], to tempt [I20]

teologal theological [II18]

teólogo theologian [erratas I]

tercería go-between [II48]

tercero go-between [I21], third [I6], another person [II62]

tercia one third [reI]

terciar to brandish [I17], to hold straight out [I20]

tercio regiment [II27], third [II64], — **y quinto** greatly [II31]

terciopelo velvet [I23]

terco stubborn [II57]

término condition [I13], boundary [I14], point [I21], limit [I24], conduct [I28], behavior [II12], word [II20], part [II51]; **en —** in conclusion [I28], — **ultramarino** maximum possible time [I6], **llegar a -s** to be on the verge [I35]

ternera veal [I2]

ternísimamente very tenderly [I41]

ternura tenderness [I20]

terradillo terrace [I40]

terrado patio [I40]

terrenal earthly [II1]

terrero bull's eye [II10]

terrón lumps of earth

tersar to smoothen [I18]

terso shiny [II7]

tesón resolve [II18]

tesoro treasury [I6], wealth [I6], treasure [I33]

testa head *Ital.* [II39]

testamento will [I6], deposition [II19]

testarudo obstinate [II53]

testigo witness [I8]

testimonio affidavit, testimony [erratas I], false testimony [I46], evidence [II23], **dar —** to prove [I20]

tez face [II39], complexion [II48]

tibiamente lukewarmly [I33]

tibio lukewarm [II20]

tiempo time [I2], occasion [II28], a — promptly [I34], in time [I35], opportunely [II68], a — que just when [II19]

tienda shop [I25], tent [II34], awning [II63]

tiento prudence [II19]; a — at random [I30], al — to the touch [I16], dar un — to take a swig [I8], a — by feel [I20], con mucho — with much groping [I20], tomar el — to estimate [II71]

tiernamente tenderly [II41]

tierno tender [I23]

tierra earth [prI], land [I1], region [I2], home [I18], ground [I22], country [I41], — firme *terra firma* [I10], echar por — to tear down [I28], perder — to give ground [II19], ir — a tierra would go along the coast [II63]

tieso stiff [II43], in good shape [II50]

tigre tiger [I32]

tijeras scissors [I29], shears [II37]

timón rudder [I41]

tinaja earthenware vat [II18]

tinelo servants' table [I37]

tinieblas darkness [I20]

tinta ink [I40]

tinte dyer's shop [II20]

tintero inkwell [I16]

tinto red wine [I35]

tiñoso scabby [I40]

tío uncle [I5]

tira strip [I26]

tirado sticking out [II43], a paso — at a brisk pace [I10]

tirador thrower [II19]

tiramira series [II35]

tiranía tyranny [I14]

tirar to throw [I3], to turn toward [I1], to pull [I16], to fire [a gun] [I39], to shoot at [II7], to print [II62]; — a to look like [I20], to lean towards [II17]

tiro shot [I9], — de ballesta a bowshot away [I9]

tirón tug [II35], stretch [II74]

titerero = titiritero puppeteer [II25]; puppet (adjective) [II26]

titubear to hesitate [I2], to waver [I34]

titulillo little title [ded. II]

título rank [prI], title [I1], caption [I9], warrant [I16], a — on pretense [I24], justo — just cause [I44]

tizona sword [I15]

toalla towel [I28], cloth [I47]

tobillo ankle [I33]

toboseco Tobosan [II18]

toca hood [II38], veil [II48]

tocado having been touched [I31]

tocado head dress [I27]

tocador handkerchief [II35], night cap [II57]

tocante a concerning [I13]

tocar to play [I2], to behoove [I2], to touch [I3], to touch on [II1], to appertain [I3], to fall to one's lot [I2], to adorn hair [I27], to concern [aprob. II]; — **a** to deal with [prI]; playing [I18]

tocar to deal with [II25], to be one's responsibility [II53], —**se** to cover one's head [II50]

tocino bacon [I25], pig to be cured [II53]

todavía always [I24], still [I52]

todo everything, **del** — complete [I6], at all [I20], entirely [I31], — **cuanto** everything [I35], **de todo en** — completely [I46]

todopoderoso almighty [I45]

togado person who wears a gown, i.e., an academic [II32]

toldo canopy [II5]

toledano Toledan [II19]

toledano from Toledo [I4]

tología theology *rustic* [II20]

tólogo theologian *rustic* [II27]

¡tomadme! look! [II21]

tomado taken [I1]

tomar to take [I1], to take on [I4], stop [as bleeding] [I34], to accept [II7], to catch [II26], —**se** to take on in a fight [II17]; — **principio** to originate [I6]

tomillo thyme [II20]

tomo importance [I46]; **de buen -** corpulent [I25]

tonante thundering [II1]

tonel cask [I6]

tono arrogance [I22], tone [II16]

tonto stupid (person) [I6], crazy [II13]

topacio topaz [II44]

topar (con) to run across [prI], to meet [I1]

toque main point [I3], blow [I15]

toquiblanco long-dressed [II48]

torcer to swerve [I9], to deflect [I9], to distort [I14], to bend [II21], to twist [II41]

torcido twisted [I22], looking away [I34], corrupt [II13]

tordesillesco from Tordesillas [II74]

tordillo dapple-grey [II16]

tormenta misfortune [I1], torture [I42/43]

tormento pain [I14], torture [I22]

tornar to return [I6], to become [I41]; — **a** to… again [I1], — **en sí** to come to [I41]

torneo tournament [I7]

torniscón punch [I25]

toro bull [I14]

torpe obscene [I40], slow mentally [I48], clumsy [II16], crude [II43]

torre turret [I2], tower [I5]

torrezno bacon [II20]

torta cake [I17]

tortolilla turtle-dove [I14]
tortolitas little turtle dove [II68]
tortuoso winding [I18]
tosca, piedra porous rock [II18]
toscano Tuscan [prI], Italian [II62]
tosco ill-bred [II32]
toser to cough [I11]
tostado sunburned [I23]
total total [II41]
trabacuenta dispute [II51]
trabado joined [I8], fierce [I35]
trabajador worker [II49]
trabajo travail [I2], difficulty [I2], tedium [I24]
trabajoso laborious [II6]
trabar to fetter [I34], to seize [I3], — **batalla** to do battle [II15], — **palabras** to dispute [I13]
trabazón connections [I42/43]
trabuco catapult [I12]
tracista schemer [I29]
tradición tradition [I41]
tradución = traducción translation[I6]
traducir to translate [I40]
tradutor translator [II5]
traduzga = traduzca translate [II3]
traer to bring [I3]
tragaderos neck [I22]
tragantón glutton [II59]
tragar to swallow [I24]
tragedia tragedy [I13]
trago swallow [I8]

tragón gluttonous [II62]
traguito bit to drink [II66]
traición, a treacherously [II32]
traídas y llevadas prostitutes [I2]
traidor traitor [I1]
traje dress [I13], attire [I24]
trama plot, woof (of cloth) [II60]
tramontana northern [I41]
trampa trap [I15]
trancar = atrancar to bar [II53]
trance peril [I3], critical moment [I27], battle [I39]
tranquilo calm [I41]
transformación transformation [II56]
tránsito stopping place [I20]
translación transformation [II22]
transparente transparent [I50]
transportado carried away [I12]
transversal side street [II26]
tranzado = trenzado braided [II20]
trapo rag [II2]
Trapobana Ceylon, now Sri Lanka [I18]
tras after [I3], behind [I6]
trasegar to decant [II54]
trasero rear [I29]
trasijado skinny [II14]
trasladar to copy [I25], to transfer [I11]
traslado copy [I51], — **a la parte** indictment [II26]
traslucirse to infer [I11], to shine through [I27], to be apparent

[II3]

trasmutación transformation [I21]

trasnochado stale [I16]

trasnochar to stay up all night [II42]

trasparente transparent [II36]

traspasar to pierce [I21], to violate [II73]

traspiés, echar to take a false step [I34]

trasponer to leave [I31]

trasponer = transponer to transport [I21]

traspuesto left [I4]

trasquilar to shear [II32]

traste fret [II46]

traste ruination [I11]

trastornado driven crazy [I48]

trastornar to overturn [II29]

trastrigo, pan de something impossible [II67]

trastrocado out of order [II32]

trastrocar to change [II29]

trastulo jokester [II7]

trasudar to sweat [I16]

trasudor sweat stain [II44]

tratamiento treatment [I23]

tratante trader [I40]

tratar to treat [I8], to discuss [I14], to address [I17], to trade [I41]; **-se** to take care of oneself [I42], **— de** to deal with [I1], **— amores** to have a love affair [I34]

trato trade [I16], dealings [I20], treatment [I49]

través: volver los ojos de — to roll one's eyes [I17]; **dar al —** to drown *fig.* I19], to overthrow [I34], **al —** over the side [II29]

travieso mischievous [II31]

traya = traiga [I14]

trayo = traigo [I10]

traza appearance [I15], plan [I22], trick [II27], instructions [II65]; **dar —** to think about [II52], to manage to [II54], to make a plan [II65]

trazar to plan [I33], to detail [I42]

trece, estar en sus to persist stubbornly [II39]

trechel brown wheat [I31]

trecho distance [I2], **de trecho en — periodically** [I25], **de trecho a — at intervals** [II58] **a —s** at intervals [I29]

tregua respite [I12], truce [I52]

tremente trembling [II21]

tremolar to wave [I52]

tres partes three fourths [I1]

tresquilado[I1] = trasquilado shorn [I7]

tresquilar = trasquilar to shear [I7]

treta wile [I26], feint (in fencing) [II14]

tribu tribe [I23]

tribulación tribulation [II11]

tribunal court [I3]

tributario person who pays tips [II49]

tributo tribute [II35]

trigo wheat [I4]

trillado well worn [II3]

trillar to thresh [I25]

trinchea = **trinchera** barricade[I39], defense [II68]

trincherar = **atrincherar** to barricade [II53]

tripas belly [I2], intestines [I8], insides [II70]

triquete step [II18], moment [II33]

triste ugly [I19]

tristemente mournfully [I5]

tristeza sadness [I18]

tristísimo very sad [I36]

triunfante triumphal [II34]

triunfar to conquer [I12]

triunfo conquest [I42/43]

trocado changed [I25]

trocar to exchange [I12], to change [I25]

troche moche, a willy-nilly [II3]

trofeo trophy [I29], monument [II27]

troglodita brute [II68]

trompar to make fun of [II43]

trompeta trumpet [I2]

tronador thundering [II41]

troncar to cut down [II7]

tronco lineage [I39], trunk of tree [I7]

trono throne [I46]

tropa crowd [I36]

tropel crowd [I4]

tropezar to stumble [I4], to trip [II4]

tropezón projection [I16]

tropiezo stumbling block [I6]

trote trot [I16]

trotico little trot [I15]

trova poem [I23]

trovador troubadour [I23]

trozo piece [I4]

trucha trout [I2]

truchuela codfish [I2]

trucos pocket billiards [I32]

truculento huge [II35]

trueco exchange [I20]; **a — de** in exchange for [I2], rather than [I33]

trueque *see* **trocar**

truhán scoundrel [I22], buffoon [II16]

trujamán narrator [II25]

truje = **traje** I brought [II4]

trujeres = **traigas** [I25]

trujeron = **trajeron** [I3]

trujiste = **trajiste** [I30]

trujo = **trajo** [I5]

tuerto injury [I2], blind in one eye [I4]

tufo aroma [I31]

tuho aroma [I31]

tullido maimed [II43]

túmulo tomb [II69]

tunda beating [II48]

tundido threadbare [I16]

tundir to shear [II41]
túnica tunic [I52]
tunicela tunic [II70]
turba mob [I10]
turbación confusion [I28]
turbado upset [I17], confused [I9]
turbamulta mish-mash [I49]
turbante turban [II23]
turbar to upset [I11], to obscure, confuse [I18], to embarrass [II7]; —se to trouble [I14], to be confused [I31], to become alarmed [I34]
turbio unclear [II61], de turbio en — becoming more and more disturbed [I1]
turco Turk [I23]
turquesa mold [II2]
turquesco Turkish [I39]
tus, tus used to call dogs [II50]
tutela protection [II38]
tutor guardian [II72]

U

ufanarse to boast [I14]
ufano proud [I33]
últimadamente finally [I42/43]
últimamente recently [reI]
último final [I20]; last one [II14]; lo — finally [I3], — fin goal [I24]
umbral threshold [II6]
una por una in any case [II65]

unción ointment [II22]
uncir to hitch [II17]
undoso undulating [II20]
ungüento ointment [I3]
único unique [I6]
universal universal [II3]
universo universe [I51]
uno a uno one at a time [I4]
untar to grease [I22], anoint [I50]
uña claw [II17], fingernail [II27], — de vaca cow's foot [II59]
urgada = hurgada worn out sexually [I5]
urgente pressing [I18]
usado customary [I27]
usanza custom [I4]
usar to make use of [I3], —se to be in use [I16], to be customary [I21]
uso custom [prI], al — fashionable [II50]
usurpado usurped [I29]
usurpar to usurp [II59]
útil useful [reI]
uva grape [II47], esta hecho — to be drunk [I45]

V

vaca beef [I1], cow [II69]
vacar to not have [II73]
vaciar to empty [I11]
vaciedad nonsense [II23]
vacilar to waver [I48]
vacío vacuum [prI], emptiness

[I33], empty [I37]

vado relief [I12], truce [II72]

vagabundo roaming [I33]; tramp [I37], vagabond [II26]

vagar to wander [II1]

vago, en in a vacuum [II17]

vaguido humor [II37], dizziness [II41], — **de cabeza** headache [I38]

vahando steaming [II47]

vaina sheath [II21], scabbard [II36]

val valley [I17]

válame Dios God bless me [I6], may God help me! [I34]

vale farewell *Lat.* [prI]

valedero binding [I16], worthy [I25]

valedor companion [II20]

valenciano of Valencia [I6]

valentía bravery [I1]

valentísimamente very valiantly [II50]

valentísimo very brave [I32], very valiant [I4]

valentón bravest man [II22]

valer to use [I1], to protect [I6], to be worth [I7], to avail [I15], to rescue [II11]

valerosísimo very valiant [II38]

valeroso brave [prI]

valía companions [II20]

valido favored [I52]

valiente brave [prI]; brave man [II17]; big [I11]

valle valley [prI]

valón Walloon [Flemish] [II18], **a la valona** with feathers [II60]

valona wide collar [II70]

valor power [I1], value [I6], worth [I24]

vanagloria boastfulness [II16]

vanaglorioso arrogant [II43]

Vandalia Andalucía [II12]

vanidad vanity [I34], foolishness [II15]

vano inane [prI], futile [I13], worthless [II51], **en —** in vain [I25]

vapulamiento flogging [I31], whipping [II35]

vapular to flog [I4]

vápulo whiplashes [II35]

vaquero cowherd [I27]

vaqueta cowhide [I49]

vaquilla heifer [II4]

vara yard *measurement* [I39], staff [I22]

varapalo staff [II27]

varazo blows with a stick [II24]

variado varied [I50]

varilla staff of office [I45]

varilla pointer [II25]

vario indifferent [I51]

varios varied [prI]

varón male [I28]

varonil manly [II35]

vasallo vassal [I24]

vasija vessel [II54]

vaso vessel [II7]

veces, todas always [I33]

vecindad nearness [I44], neighborly [II27]

vecino neighbor [I4], resident [I4]

vedija tuft [I23]

veduño grapevine [II38]

vee = **ve** [I20]

veedor inspector [I22]

vegada time [I46]

vehemencia violence [I15], forcefulness [II5]

vehemente keen [I23]

veinte 20 [II14]

vejez old age [I28]

vejiga bladder [II11]

vejote old man [II23]

vela watching over [I3]; candle [I3]; sail [I15]

velar staying awake [I2]; to watch over [I3], to stay awake [II20]

velarte broadcloth [I1]

veleta weathervane [I52]

vello body hair [I35]

vellorí ordinary broadcloth [I1]

velloso hairy [II1]

velludo velvet [I1]

velo veil [I27]

vena vein [I42/43]

venablo spear [II34]

vencedor conqueror [I18], conquering [II69]

vencejos swift [bird] [II53]

vencer to conquer [I1], to win [I18]

vencido subdued [I14], conquered [I16]

vencimiento victory [I33], vanquishment [I8]

venda blindfold [prI]

vendar to bandage [I11], to blindfold [II41]

vendible sellable [I48]

venecianos Venetians [I39]

veneno venom [II46]

veneno poison [I22], venom [II11]

venenoso poisonous [II65]

venenoso poisonous [I14]

venerable venerable [II20]

veneración veneration [II8]

venerando venerable [II31]

vengado avenged [I17]

venganza vengeance [I10]

vengar(se) to avenge (oneself) [I7]

vengativo vindictive [I27]

venia forgiveness [I6]

venida arrival [I2]

venidero future [I2], coming [I37]

venir to come [I25]; — **a ser** to become [I7], — **en** to agree [I6], to consent [I27], — **en conocimiento** to come to know [I13], — **a sacar** to gather [I49], — **bien con** to fit in [II18], **por** — future [II19], —**le más a cuento** to be more opportune [II70]

venta inn [I2]

ventaja superiority [I27], advantage [II24], supplementary soldier's income [II24], **hacer —** to surpass [I21], **yo llevo de —** to have in addition [I18]

ventana window [I6]

ventanilla little window [I40]

venteril pertaining to an innkeeper [I3]

ventero innkeeper [I2]

ventrera belt [II60]

ventura fortune [prI], happiness [I15], luck [I40], **por —** by chance [I18], luck [I22], **sin —** unfortunate [I29]

venturoso fortunate [I16], lucky [I18], happy [I36]

verano summer [I41], **a lo de —** in cool clothes [II72]

veras reality [II35], realities [I45], truths [I48], **de —** truly [I18], in earnest [I41], **con más —** even more [I4], **con las —** earnestly [I24]

verdad truth [prI]

verdaderamente truly [I2]

verdadero true [I1], sincere [I42], truthful [II64], right [II65]

verde green [I2]

verdugado hoopskirt [II5], **— redondo** bell-shaped skirt [II50]

verdugo executioner [I22], scourge [I39]

verdura greenness [I50]

vereda path [II34]

veredes *arch.* **veréis** you will see [I8]

vergonzoso shy [II21]

vergüenza shame [I29], timidity [II58], public punishment [I22]

vericueto rough road [II5]

verídico truthful [II41]

verificarse to be verified [II28]

verisímil = verosímil credible [II24]

verisimilitud= verosimilitud credibility [I47]

verja grate [I33], bar [I47]

verosímil credible [I1]

verruga wart [II14]

versado versed [I6]

verse to find oneself [I2], **— con** to confront [I45]

verso line of poetry [I5], poetry [I6], **— mayor** verse longer than 8 syllables

verter to shed [I14]

vestido dress [I11], outfit [I51]; dressed [dedI]; **—s** garments [I27], clothing [I31]

vestidura garment [I25]

vestiglo horrid monster [I19]

vestir to wear [I42], **—se** to dress [prI]

veta vein [I33]

vez, otra again [I4], **de una —** at once [I6], **tal —** sometimes

[II45]

vía way [I18], road [II26]

vía = **veía** [I4]

viaje trip [I7]

víame = **veíame** [I22]

víamos = **veíamos** [I23]

vían = **veían** [I28]

viandantes passer by [II58]

viandas food [I10]

víbora viper [I14]

vicario vicar [II38], **general**
vicar-general, bishop's adm.
deputy [aprob. II]

vicio vice [I48], **de** — without
reason [II55]

vicioso luxuriant [I25], luxurious
[I51], vicious [II6], depraved
[II32]

victorioso victorious [II34]

vida life [I23]

vido = **vio** [I22]

vidrio glass [I33]

vidro = **vidrio** glass [I16]

viejo old person [I5]

viento wind [I8], **papar** — to
waste time [II31]

vientre stomach [I31], womb
[I46]

viernes Friday [I2]

viga beam [I49], log [II51]

vigilancia watchfulness [II12]

vigilante wakeful [II23]

vigilia loss of sleep [I38],
wakefulness [II68]

vigor energy [I3]

vigüela vihuela, guitar-like
instrument [II12]

vil despicable [I8]

vileza vile deed [I25]

vilezas depravity [I34]

villa town [dedI]

villancico carol [I12]

villanería low birth [II43]

villanía foul name [I31]

villano rustic [I4], wicked person
[I9]

vino wine [I2]

viña vineyard [I25]

viperina snake [I30]

vira welt of shoe [II38]

virote one's own business [II14]

virrey viceroy [I40]

virtud power [I3], righteousness
[I12], virtue [I14]

virtuoso virtuous [II16]

visaje facial expression [I42], face
[I46]

visera visor [I2]

visión vision [I46]

visita visit [II63]

vislumbre semblance [I16],
glittering [I2]

visorrey viceroy [I47]

víspera(s) on the eve of [II4],
vespers [II20]

vista sight [I14], vision [I18],
appearance [II1], in sight of
[I30], inspection [II45], **corto de**
— short sighted [I49], **a** —**s** to
be seen [II62], **a** — **de** visible

[II62]

visto seen [I7], **no** — unheard of [I25]

vistoso beautiful [I29], handsome [II14]

vitoria = **victoria** triumph [I7]

vituperar to condemn [II39], to censure [I51], to abuse [II60]

vituperio reproach [I27]

vituperoso censured [II40]

viuda widow [I3]

viudo widower [I26]

vivienda life style [I31]

viviente living [I13]

vivo alive [I4], intense [I20], **al** — vividly [I1]

vizcaíno Basque [I8]

Vizcaya Basque country [I18]

vizconde viscount [dedI]

voacé you [I22]

vobis: de — **vobis** free [I30]

vocablo word [II12]

vocación name [II8]

vocear to cry [I27]

vocería yelling [II34]

voces shouts [I5], **dar** — to shout [I3], **a** — shouting [I5]

volado blown up [II24]

volandas, en in an instant [I49]

volandillas, en in the air [I31]

volar to fly [I6], to blow up [I40], **como** — something impossible [II44]

volatería flight [I46], hawking [II34]

volátiles, cosas poultry [I10]

volcar = **revolcar** to wallow [I5]

voleo volley [II70]

voltario fickle [II14]

volteado turned [I8]

volteador acrobat [II22]

voltear to whirl [I18], to tumble [II22]

voluntad will [I4], love [I27], confidence [I33], affection [I24], good will [I42], **mala** — indisposed [I48], **a su** — any way they see fit [II74]

volver to turn into [I6], to return [I7], to turn over [I8], to translate [I9], to wheel (a horse around) [I13], to change [I25], to turn towards [II17], to turn [II40]; —**se** to turn into [I14], — **las espaldas** to turn around [I14], — **los ojos de través** to roll one's eyes [I17], — **en sí** to come to [I21], — **loco** to drive crazy [I22], —**se loco** to go crazy [I42/43], to defend [II37]

vomitar to vomit [I16]

vómito vomiting [II12]

voquible = **vocablo** word [II3]

vos you *sing.* [reI], *archaic* **os** to you [I2]

votar to swear [I18]

voto supplication [I8], vow [I21], vote [I45]; — **a tal** by Jove! [prI], — **a Dios** I swear to God [I10]

voz voice [I1], public opinion [I29], shout [I36]; **a media —** in a whisper [I4]

vuelo flight [I23]

vuelta return [I27], turn [II7], **dar la —** to return [I44], **dar una — a la redonda** to mind one's own business [I22], **a la —** just around [I24], **la — de** towards [I41]

vuelto turned [I8], turned into [I18], **— en sí** having come to [II27]

vuesa merced your grace *rustic* [II17]

vuestra merced your grace [I1]

vulgo public [prI]

Y

ya sometimes [II17], now [I23], even [II67]; **—... ya...** either... or [II69], **— que** even when [I10], as soon as [I17], even if [I31]

yacer to lie [I8]

yago I lie *from* **yacer** [I15]

yangüés person from the town of Yanguas [I10]

yantar *arch.* to eat [I2]; dinner [I7]

yedra ivy [I11]

yegua mare [I4]

yelmo helmet [I10]

yelo = hielo ice [I13]

yema de un dedo fingertip [I26]

yerba herb [I10], grass [I15]

yermo wilderness [I28]

yerno son-in-law [II26]

yerra, se makes a mistake (from **errar**) [I20]

yerro error [I20]

yeso plaster [I33]

yogar *arch.* to lie [II45]

yogo yoke [I46]

Z

zabullir = zambullir to plunge [II20]

zafio ignorant [I23], coarse [II19]

zaga, irle [quedarle] en not to be far behind [I1]

zagal young man [I11]

zagaleja young woman [I11]

zahareño wild [I20]

zaheriendo = zahiriendo [*from* **zaherir**] censuring [I12]

zahurda pigsty [II70]

zalá prayer *Arab.* [I40]

zalea undressed sheepskin [I11]

zalema salaam [I40]

zamarro sheepskin jacket [II53]

zamorano Zamoran [II20]

zampoña pastoral flute [II73]

zanahoria carrot [II55]

zanca shank [I9]

zancadilla, echarle una to trip someone [II60]

zancajo heelbone, **roer los —s** to backbite [II36]

zángano drone bee [II49]

zanja foundation trench [II20]

zapateador rustic dancer19]

zapatear to dance while slapping shoes [II62]

zapatero shoemaker [I15]

zapateta caper [I25]

zapatico little shoe [I52]

zapatilla fencing foil button [II19], slipper [II38]

zapato shoe [I4]

zaque wineskin [I11]

zaquizamí garret [II67]

zarandajas trifles [II23]

zarpar el ferro to weigh anchor [II63]

zarzas brambles [I50]

zarzo canopy support [II11]

zas whack [I37]

zoca en colodra, de from one place to another [I18]

zorra fox [II38]

zorruno foxlike [II38]

zuecos clogs [II5]

zumbar to buzz [I23]

zurdo left-handed [I18]

zurrón pouch [I24]

zuzar = azuzar to urge [I52]